The Black Arch

FACE THE RAVEN

By Sarah Groenewegen

Published June 2018 by Obverse Books

Cover Design © Cody Schell

Text © Sarah Groenewegen, 2018

Range Editors: Paul Simpson, Philip Purser-Hallard

Editor: Kara Dennison

Sarah would like to thank:

Simon Belcher for his research into where the trap street might be in London, Simon Guerrier for his advice, Kara for her editorial skills, Philip for his patience, Steven Moffat for his vision of **Doctor Who***, and Sarah Dollard for talking to me about her amazing story.*

Also Available

For my brother, Stephen, for the many hours we spent as children talking about **Doctor Who** to work out what makes it tick.

In memory of my mother, Eileen Jennifer (1940-2018) and my father, Peter (1939-2018). Travelling together.

CONTENTS

OVERVIEW

Serial Title: *Face the Raven*

Writer: Sarah Dollard

Director: Justin Molotnikov

Original UK Transmission Date: 21 November 2015

Running Time: 46m 53s

UK Viewing Figures: 6.0 million

Regular Cast: Peter Capaldi (The Doctor), Jenna Coleman (Clara)

Recurring Cast: Maisie Williams (Ashildr), Joivan Wade (Rigsy)

Guest Cast: Naomi Ackie (Jen), Simon Manyonda (Kabel), Simon Paisley Day (Rump), Letitia Wright (Anahson), Robin Soans (Chronolock Guy), Angela Clerkin (Alien Woman), Caroline Boulton (Habrian Woman), Jenny Lee (Elderly Woman)

Antagonists: Ashildr, the Raven.

Sequels and Prequels: *Heaven Sent* (TV, 2015), *Hell Bent* (TV, 2015).

Responses:

'[*Face the Raven*] feels like an episode of television you could only ever see on **Doctor Who**. A heady mixture of science fiction, Gothic whodunit and emotional rollercoaster, it doesn't just leave you breathless – it leaves you wanting more.'

[Jon Cooper, *The Independent*, 21 November 2015]

'But after all the scrapes they've been in, what befalls Clara in *Face the Raven* is unmomentous, unspectacular; the stakes are small.

Couldn't she have died saving the universe?'

[Patrick Mulkern, *Radio Times*, 21 November 2015]

SYNOPSIS

Clara's friend **Rigsy**, now living in London with his girlfriend and baby, calls to ask for Clara's help. He has awoken with no memory of the previous day, and what appears to be a tattoo, showing a number which is counting down by the minute. **The Doctor** establishes that Rigsy has been given an amnesia drug after contact with aliens, and that the tattoo signals the time he has left to live. Seeking possible locations for alien life in central London, the three consider 'trap streets' – fake streets inserted into maps to detect copyright violation – and discover an alley in central London, hidden from ordinary perception. Data recovered from Rigsy's phone suggests that he was called the previous morning, presumably to be summoned to the trap street.

The street turns out to be a refuge giving asylum to aliens of many species, all appearing human thanks to the telepathic field that hides it. Its 'Mayor' is **Ashildr**, aka Lady Me, a Viking who the Doctor made immortal over a thousand years previously[1]. She maintains order between the hostile occupants by means of a Quantum Shade: 'chronolocks' such as Rigsy's tattoo constitute a death sentence to be carried out by the Shade in the form of a **Raven**. During his missing time Rigsy was convicted of the murder of a female (and therefore psychic) Janus refugee named **Anah**, whose body Ashildr now keeps in stasis.

Clara learns from **Rump**, one of the street's denizens, that Rigsy's sentence may be commuted either by having the chronolock lifted by the Shade's master, or through passing it on to a willing recipient.

---

[1] *The Girl Who Died* (2015).

Clara, who Ashildr has guaranteed her personal protection, persuades him to give her his chronolock. She also realises that Anah's son, **Anahson**, is actually a daughter, and thus psychic like her mother. Anahson confirms the Doctor's suspicion that Ashildr has used Rigsy's abduction experience as a 'mystery' to draw him to the street. The Doctor discovers that Anah is alive and releases her from stasis – but only by activating a mechanism which steals the TARDIS key and locks a teleport bracelet to his arm.

Her trap sprung, Ashildr offers to lift Rigsy's chronolock, and is horrified to discover that Clara now has it. This has removed Ashildr's ability to rescind the death sentence, and it cannot now be escaped. After making the Doctor promise not to take revenge on Ashildr or the Street's inhabitants, Clara steps out into the street to face the Raven, which kills her.

Ashildr activates the teleport and the Doctor vanishes. Some time later, Rigsy completes a street art tribute to Clara, painted on the abandoned TARDIS.

INTRODUCTION

'[Desire] is the drive towards satisfying something which is ultimately unsatisfiable.'

[Patrick Fuery][2].

Face the Raven is the first of three stories – continuing with *Heaven Sent* and *Hell Bent* (all 2015) – which begin with the Doctor and Clara joyously sharing a wild adventure, then chart a tragic miscalculation by Clara that leads to her death, and the capture of the Doctor by the Time Lords. The trilogy is unusual for **Doctor Who** in that the first of the episodes was written by new-to-the-series Sarah Dollard, and the final two by head writer Steven Moffat.

At the core of *Face the Raven* is the collision of Clara and Ashildr's personal motives concerning the Doctor, resulting in Clara's death.

Clara's twinned desires for consequence-free adventure and to emulate her hero and friend, the Doctor, lead to the tragedy of her death in this first story. She believes she will be safe because she always has been safe – until she discovers that her assumption of Rigsy's death sentence is irreversible. Clara believes she is as clever as the Doctor, that she has anticipated and accounted for each and every move made by Ashildr in her plan to ensnare the Doctor; only Clara hasn't, of course. Clara's desire to be like the Doctor collapses the outside signs that she has been successful in realising that desire – as seen most clearly in *Flatline* (2014) – into her mistaken belief that she really has become as clever as him.

Ashildr, too, is driven in *Face the Raven* by a desire: to keep the Earth

---

[2] Fuery, Patrick, *Theories of Desire*, p22.

safe from the Doctor. More than likely, it's this desire that motivates her to accept the Time Lords' contract. In that sense, she is the Doctor's antagonist in the story, but she is far from an archetypal villain. She has built a sanctuary for aliens, both wronged and wrong-uns, hidden in a trap street in central London. She rules it brutally, showing a ruthlessness in her desire to negate what she sees as the effects of the Doctor's hubris. While that desire motivates her, the Doctor is not her only waking obsession.

Mary Ann Doane began her study of 1940s women's films by looking at Woody Allen's *The Purple Rose of Cairo* (1985). Allen's film is all about the interplay between desire and reality: Mia Farrow's character calls to life a character from a movie she is watching. She has desired him, a fictional character, to become real. Doane's contention was that Allen's movie could only have had a woman make real a fantasy the way Farrow's character does. Doane argued 'there is a certain naïveté assigned to women in relation to systems of signification – a tendency to deny the process of representation, to collapse the opposition between the sign (the image) and the real. To "misplace" desire by attaching it too securely to representations'[3]. Or, as cultural theorist Clare Whatling put it, 'Women [...] do not possess the ability to distinguish between image and reality'[4]. Farrow's character over-identifies with the film-within-a-film, which in turn allows her to realise her desire.

Doctor Who is a series of contradictions, particularly of the everyday

---

[3] Doane, Mary Ann, *The Desire to Desire: The Women's Films of the 1940s*, p1.
[4] Whatling, Clare, *Screen Dreams: Fantasising Lesbians in Film*, pp56-57.

and extraordinary. From the very first story, *An Unearthly Child* (1963), the audience sees what was then the normal sight of a police call box opening up into an impossibly large and futuristic control room; that moment sets one of the consistent contradictions that both Clara and Ashildr embody in *Face the Raven*. Clara is the most ordinary of 'impossible girls' who wants to be like the Doctor, and Ashildr is an innocent made immortal by the Doctor who becomes more like the Doctor than Clara can ever be.

That first **Doctor Who** story also set the other constant and contradictory feature of the series; it is a series about departures and arrivals. *Face the Raven* sees the return of both Rigsy and Ashildr, while Ashildr's trap instigates the departure of both Clara and the Doctor. Further, the story is also about escape(ism) and shelter for the monsters and aliens in the Doctor's history – new and old.

CHAPTER 1: THE IMPOSSIBLE GIRL

'Let me be brave, let me be brave...'

[Clara][5]

Clara Oswald is more than her death, which comes at the climax of *Face the Raven*. She remains one of the strangest companions in the whole history of **Doctor Who**, both in the narrative of the series as shown and in the metatext of the series' production. Before exploring Clara Oswald's death in *Face the Raven*, we need to understand how her arrival set her character and her relationships with all the Doctors, and her role as a unique companion in **Doctor Who**'s history.

In essence, the character of Clara Oswald served a particular narrative function for a significant milestone in television history: the 50th anniversary of **Doctor Who**. For the vast and diverse audience the show attracts, she had to be both familiar, to provide a nostalgic link to the whole history of the series, as well as different enough to be interesting. She also witnessed the regeneration of the 11th Doctor into the 12th, and therefore serves as a bridge for the audience between the familiar and new. Plus, she is one of a small number of companions who died while adventuring with the Doctor.

Soufflé Girl

'REMEMBER ME FOR WE SHALL MEET AGAIN.'

[Clara Oswin Oswald's gravestone, *The Snowmen* (2012)]

---

[5] All quotes from *Face the Raven* unless otherwise noted.

The tension between the old and new is an ongoing manifestation of what John Tulloch called the similar-but-different essence of **Doctor Who**[6]. That tension existed from the opening scenes of the first episode, 'An Unearthly Child' (1963), as the police officer on his beat strolled past the junkyard that housed a police call box that isn't, and isn't where it should be, as the audience in 1963 Britain would have known. This tension exists in every story of **Doctor Who** in various and often multiple ways, mostly through the contemporary human companion or companions travelling with the alien Doctor (and sometimes with other aliens). It is present in everyday objects – Bluetooth earpieces[7], shop mannequins[8], a raven – being used by the alien monsters, usually to inflict destruction. That sight of everyday objects acting as they shouldn't brings the audience not only fear, but a unique thrill. As the show itself has grown older it has picked over familiar tropes to reassure its audience that it is the same series, but usually with twists and new takes to keep their interest from waning and to attract new audiences. Old friends and monsters often reappear, either in flashback scenes or featuring in new stories. In the case of Clara Oswald, she is inserted into the narrative of the entire series to bring forth nostalgic glimpses of the past.

Clara arrived for the 50th anniversary; for that, she had to be both similar enough to what had come before to not scare parts of the audience away, and different enough to attract and retain those in the audience who enjoy novelty. **Doctor Who** by 2013 was an

---

[6] Tulloch, John, 'Dr Who: Similarity and Difference', *The Australian Journal of Screen Theory*, #11 & 12 (1982), pp8–26.
[7] *Rise of the Cybermen / The Age of Steel* (2006).
[8] *Spearhead from Space* (1970), *Rose* (2005).

institution heavy with history, and popular world-wide. The 50th anniversary story, *The Day of the Doctor* (2013), entered *The Guinness Book of Records* as the largest ever simulcast of a television drama[9]. The British news media always report on changes in TARDIS crew, as do the their counterparts in countries around the world where **Doctor Who** has become a television stalwart. That media interest poses a risk of spoiling surprises, and the **Doctor Who** production team has struggled on numerous occasions to manage leaks of story details. Steven Moffat, lead writer and producer between 2010 and 2017, often exhorted journalists and audiences at previews to not run stories or post details online that would spoil surprises in the narrative.

Audiences knew that Amy Pond and Rory Williams were leaving just before the 50th anniversary, and inevitably a replacement companion would be found. Following the familiar pattern, the casting of the new companion made the news, and the image of Jenna-Louise Coleman as Clara Oswald became familiar to audiences during 2012[10]. However, this was the start of the metatextual game that led from 2012 into the 50th anniversary year.

On 1 September 2012, BBC One aired *Asylum of the Daleks* to open series 7, a series split into 'A' and 'B' halves over the course of two years. This story featured Amy and Rory, and Matt Smith as the 11th Doctor, and immediately after the opening credits the audience saw a face familiar from publicity about the new companion. But we learn

---

[9] Guerrier, Simon, Steve O'Brien and Ben Morris, *Whographica: An Infographic Guide to Space and Time*, pp204-205. That record was broken by **CSI: Crime Scene Investigation** in 2015.
[10] She shortened her name in 2013 to Jenna Coleman.

quickly that this isn't Clara. It's Oswin Oswald, and she is trying to make soufflés in the crashed survival pod of the star-liner *Alaska*, surrounded by insane Daleks. As the adventure progresses, we learn Oswin Oswald is bisexual, but then came the big reveal: she is a Dalek. Not a puppet, but a fully formed Dalek struggling against that fact. She helps the Doctor, Amy and Rory to physically escape from the planet, and heroically she wipes the Daleks' minds about the Doctor. Whoever Oswin Oswald was as a human is destroyed; even in the world of **Doctor Who**, there is no saving her. Clearly, Jenna-Louise Coleman as Oswin Oswald is not the new companion.

Then, on Christmas Day 2012, Moffat and the production team pulled off the same trick in *The Snowmen*. Jenna-Louise Coleman returns, this time playing a barmaid called Clara Oswald working at the Rose and Crown pub in 1892. She leads a double life as Miss Montague, governess to the Latimer family. When the Doctor meets her, he, like the audience, is astonished. Her talk of soufflés and telling him to run echo the Oswin Oswald who helped him, Amy and Rory escape the Daleks and their asylum. She is clearly the same woman, but it's impossible.

Even without this mystery, she wins the Doctor over by being the first to exclaim how the TARDIS is smaller on the outside rather than larger on the inside. Surely, audiences were thinking, this must be the new companion to replace Amy and Rory. But then in front of the Doctor, Vastra, Jenny and Strax, this Clara Oswald is killed to save humanity and the Earth. As though for emphasis, her gravestone is shown at the end of the story and reads: 'CLARA OSWIN OSWALD. REMEMBER ME FOR WE SHALL MEET AGAIN. BORN NOVEMBER 23,

1866. DIED DECEMBER 24, 1892[11].' Obviously, the 23 November date is meant as a nostalgic chime with those in the audience who know the date when the first episode of **Doctor Who** was first broadcast, and a primer for the 50th anniversary celebrations in the coming year.

Clara Oswald returns in *The Bells of Saint John* (2013). That story begins with the Doctor in 1207 trying to divine the nature of this enigmatic young woman he has now met twice, and who has sacrificed herself twice to save him and, to greater or lesser extents, humanity. The mystery deepens when in contemporary London 24-year-old Clara Oswald calls him herself, in expectation of a computer helpdesk[12]. The Doctor recognises her as his 'soufflé girl' who tells him to run at the most apposite moments. He stalks her across her time stream and discovers her family during *The Rings of Akhaten* (2013), which is otherwise set in an alien planetary system. Clara's mother is Ellie, who was born on 11 September 1960 and died on 5 March 2005[13]. Her father is Dave. At the end of *Journey to the Centre of the TARDIS* (2013) the Doctor interrogates Clara Oswald about Oswin Oswald and Clara Oswin Oswald, and Clara insists she knows nothing about either of them. That point is emphasised by Jenny

---

[11] The date of her birth is 97 years before the first episode of **Doctor Who** was first broadcast; the date of her death is 120 years before the broadcast of that Christmas story; the birthday of the Victorian Clara is also 120 years before Clara Oswald's birth as established in *Death in Heaven* (2014).

[12] Thanks, as we eventually learn in *Death in Heaven*, to the machinations of Missy.

[13] 21 days before **Doctor Who** returned with *Rose*.

during *The Crimson Horror* (2013) when she meets Clara for the second time, but Clara has no knowledge of Jenny, Vastra or Strax. Clara's curiosity about herself and the Doctor's obsession with her is piqued when on her return home to the children she nannies, Angie and Artie, she sees them looking at pictures of her in 1974[14], 1983[15], and 1892[16]. Of course, she does not recognise the last photograph, further underlining the strangeness of her existence.

What's actually remarkable about Clara is that she is just an ordinary young woman living and working in contemporary London. She's sharp, sarcastic, with a drive to help others where she can. By *Cold War* (2013) – **her** third adventure with the Doctor, but the fifth time the audience had seen her or someone very like her – she understands the dangers and horrors, but observes at the end of that tale that saving the world is what they do. That ultimate drive to save others off-sets the trauma of seeing death first-hand, but her fear is real. The conundrum throughout 2013 is the Doctor knowing there is more to Clara, there has to be, while all the clues point to the conclusion that there is not in fact anything more about her as a person.

The mystery is solved in *The Name of the Doctor* (2013) when she runs into the Doctor's time stream to save him from the Great Intelligence, fracturing herself throughout his history. The suggestion is that Oswin Oswald and Clara Oswin Oswald were both splinters of Clara. Audiences keyed for the 50th anniversary were able to see flashbacks to each previous Doctor, revisiting Time Lord lore before

---

[14] *Hide* (2013).
[15] *Cold War* (2013).
[16] *The Snowmen.*

watching *The Day of the Doctor* on the actual anniversary.

Witness to a Regeneration

'I'm Clara Oswald. I'm the impossible girl. I was born to save the Doctor.'

[Clara, *The Name of the Doctor*]

As a **Doctor Who** companion, Clara is unique in that she is central to anniversary stories that are revelatory about the Doctor and his origins. She is one of a few who dies, and she witnesses a regeneration. In this last she is the bridge for audiences for multiple events that, to new fans, may be especially confusing. Through her reaction to the regeneration, we can see traits in her character and her relationship with the Doctor that drive the narrative in *Face the Raven*.

Doctor Who is an unusual television series in that for all its action-adventure trappings, the backstory for the titular character has evolved over a long time. Most fiction series have a main character, or group of characters, whose history is known at least in a rudimentary manner by the audience in the first few stories. Part of their lives may be shrouded in mystery for a relatively short while, but only to create dramatic tension before the secret is revealed. This approach is a key to audience identification, and is a standard requirement of popular fiction, especially that aimed at children. **Doctor Who** was ostensibly a children's fantasy series that has been described as essentially a 'hero story'[17]. However, **Doctor Who** is not

---

[17] For example, Tulloch, John and Manuel Alvarado, *Doctor Who: The Unfolding Text* and Hourihan, Margery, *Deconstructing the Hero: Literary Theory and Children's Literature.*

and never has been that simple to describe. Margery Hourihan points out that 'the most obvious feature of the hero story is that it is **his** story'. She further argues that the narrative point of view in this sort of story-telling is vital in establishing the right character as the hero[18]. **Doctor Who** subverts that story-telling technique for hero tales; in **Doctor Who** the companions are the intended characters with whom audiences identify, rather than the Doctor, and yet the Doctor is ostensibly the hero. Companions aren't sidekicks, and outside a few stories since the series returned in 2005 do not fulfil a narrator role in the model of ancient Greek plays, or Watson to Sherlock Holmes. The key to understanding the Doctor-companion dynamic is in understanding the Doctor as an alien being who is friends with a companion who is human. As Tulloch and Alvarado say, the Doctor is 'an alien, an outsider'[19], even if the producers would paradoxically appeal to audiences by selling the series on the strength of its star, the actor playing the part[20]. The Doctor is always shrouded in mystery, always an alien[21]. In contrast, the companions were usually from Earth and from a time contemporary to the audience. This dynamic is precisely that of Clara and both her Doctors.

Doctor Who is a series of departures and arrivals and the linked tension of home and escape. 'An Unearthly Child' is all about these paradoxical tensions that permeate throughout the show's history, and are one of the reasons for its longevity. Two teachers, Ian Chesterton and Barbara Wright, follow one of their students, the

---

[18] Hourihan, *Deconstructing the Hero*, p38 (her emphasis).
[19] Tulloch and Alvarado, *The Unfolding Text*, p47.
[20] Tulloch and Alvarado, *The Unfolding Text*, pp196-197.
[21] Tulloch and Alvarado, *The Unfolding Text*, footnote on p328.

enigmatic Susan Foreman, home to a police box incongruously located in a junkyard. Here we discover that Susan and her 'grandfather', the Doctor, have departed their home in mysterious circumstances, and at the conclusion of this first episode Ian and Barbara depart their London home to begin their adventures. Three years later, due to ill health, William Hartnell announced his retirement from the series. Patrick Troughton arrived with the concept of regeneration, and many other actors have subsequently filled the role of the Doctor when the previous actor departed. Troughton's departure saw the arrival of the Time Lords, the Doctor's people finally being revealed after six years. Producers, actors, concepts — all these have continued to depart and arrive over the 55 years since the show began. That includes the roles of the Doctor and of his companions, and their relationships.

Much of **Doctor Who** revolves around the companions, even if obliquely, because they are the audience identification point. There are only a few ways companions leave the Doctor[22]. Most often they are forced to leave, or leave because they want to go home, or just stop the roller-coaster ride, or to help others, or because they've found love, or to embark on adventures on their own. These reasons are reused, albeit with little twists. Donna Noble wasn't the first companion to have her mind wiped of her adventures with the Doctor, but her fate was played for tragic horror rather than the pained regret for Jamie and Zoe when they were forced to leave decades earlier[23]. This is another example of familiar tropes keeping

---

[22] Guerrier et al, *Whographica*, pp100-101.
[23] *The War Games* (1969), *The Five Doctors* (1983), *The Stolen Earth / Journey's End* (2008).

the established audience tuning in, but these are new experiences for the newer characters and newer audiences alike. The joy is in experiencing the wonders of the TARDIS, and the familiar-yet-alien nature of the Doctor, for the first time, and then discovering the dark realities of the danger. For all that, there is an apparent and reassuring safety in the horror and excitement. **Doctor Who** has a quality about it like an oft-told fairy tale. Scary, unsettling, but it becomes comforting in its repeated familiarity.

Given that **Doctor Who** is an adventure series with many characters facing deadly peril week-in week-out, it would be surprising if none of the companions ever died. Two short-term companions, Katarina and Sara Kingdom, died in the 12-part story *The Daleks' Master Plan* (1965-66), but it was not until 1982 that a well-established companion, Adric, did so[24]. Like Clara, Adric had served as an anchor for the audience during a regeneration, in his case of Tom Baker's fourth Doctor into Peter Davison's fifth[25]. Unlike Clara, Adric joined the Doctor by stowing away on board the TARDIS, escaping from a place he didn't want to be. Although he looked like a human teenager, Adric was an alien like the Doctor: he was a mathematical genius, and of a race that had the ability to regenerate, at least partially[26]. However, while he originally craved escape, Adric begins his last story by wanting to go home; instead, by the end of the story

---

[24] *Earthshock* (1982). In *Face the Raven*, while the Doctor is searching for the trap street and counting out loud he reaches 82 and instructs a young boy to 'remember 82'. This would be in keeping with other obscure numerical references in recent series.
[25] *Logopolis* (1981), *Castrovalva* (1982).
[26] *Full Circle* (1980).

he has sacrificed himself to save the Earth from the Cybermen[27].

There are parallels between Adric and Clara in how both evince certain behavioural similarities with the Doctor. Both are the bridges for the audience watching a regeneration; they are the common points of reference through which the audience can identify as we all mourn the loss of an old friend and are introduced to a new person. That person enters life traumatically, and it always takes time for the Doctor to adjust to the new body and develop unique personality quirks, as well as settle into the same person the character has always been: that essential Doctor-ness the audience knows and loves.

Clara struggles with the change, and to be fair the Doctor following this regeneration is a challenge. By the time Clara met and got to know the 11th Doctor he was more eccentric than outright alien, but the 12th Doctor is more alien than merely eccentric. That alien strand diminishes to a degree, but never leaves, and the 12th Doctor is difficult to regard as human throughout all the stories in which he appears. Physically, the Doctor has always looked human although he is alien. Indeed, the Doctor has always looked like a white man (or, very recently, a white woman[28]): but the Doctor's 'body just seemed to be something he went about in; a concessionary formality to stop the rest of physical reality getting even more confused'[29]; a line from the novel *Lungbarrow* (1997) that neatly encapsulates the fundamental concept of regeneration.

Regeneration is akin to death and renewal of an adult form. It is what

---

[27] *Earthshock.*
[28] *Twice Upon a Time* (2017).
[29] Platt, Marc, *Lungbarrow*, p106.

starkly marks the Doctor as different from his human companions. However, as with Adric and his ability to partially regenerate, there are narrative echoes of the Doctor's regenerative capability in Clara. Clara was initially introduced as a mystery who sacrifices herself repeatedly to save the Doctor as well as others[30]. After we learn that these other Oswalds, all played by Jenna Coleman, are among the fractured versions of her once she ran into the Doctor's time stream[31], Clara's life is reset. When *The Day of the Doctor* begins, she is no longer a governess or nanny but a teacher at Coal Hill School, the school being one of many nostalgic hooks back to 'An Unearthly Child' and other moments in the show's long history.

This Clara is the same yet different to the Clara who sacrificed herself in *The Name of the Doctor*. She is clearly the same person, with the same name and mannerisms. She knows what to do with UNIT. She tells the Doctor at the end that she knows when he needs to be left alone, which emphasises just how well she knows him. But, her life is different to what it was between *The Bells of Saint John* and *The Name of the Doctor*. She lives alone in a flat on an estate in London's south-east, there are only fleeting references to her life before she threw herself into the Doctor's timeline, and there are some details that jar. Her family as established in *The Rings of Akhaten* are different to those seen at Christmas in *The Time of the Doctor* (2013), with a father who looks different[32], a grandmother and her father's partner Linda, but no mention of Clara's beloved mother, Ellie. The changes are far from as extreme as seen in the Doctor's

---

[30] Although perhaps not as many times as Rory Williams.
[31] *The Name of the Doctor*.
[32] Dave Oswald was played by two actors, Michael Dixon and James Buller.

regenerations, but they are suggestive of a similar type of character rejuvenation to suit changes in the narrative.

Bizarre Love Triangle

DOCTOR

Am I a good man?

CLARA

I don't know.

[*Into the Dalek* (2014)]

Following the Doctor's regeneration, and Clara's difficulty in coming to terms with the changes in her friend's physical form and behaviour, she falls in love with fellow teacher Danny Pink. We see elements of the blossoming relationship through the stories following *Into the Dalek*, but the two main stories that deal with Clara and Danny, and their relationship with the Doctor, are *Listen* and *The Caretaker* (both 2014).

Listen switches between Clara on her disastrous dinner date with Danny where they both make judgements and assumptions and banter with unfunny jokes, and Clara accompanying the Doctor as he sorts out a universal nightmare. The two story strands highlight the emotional seesaw that Clara tries and fails to balance between the Doctor and Danny; it is only because she doesn't actually fall from that seesaw that she thinks she succeeds. Clara's inability to focus fully on either story strand muddles her thoughts, leading them from the bedroom of a young Danny (né Rupert) to the literal end of the universe... and finally to the Doctor's own childhood, tying up a stray thread from the anniversary stories.

Clara's relationship with the Doctor is revealed to Danny during *The Caretaker*. During and following that story, Danny challenges Clara repeatedly over the artifice of herself she has created in defence against all the stress adventuring with the Doctor has accumulated in her. He sees the bad effects of the Doctor's hold on her, and likens the Doctor to a superior and callous class-bound army officer. The Doctor is all but blind to Danny's growing role in Clara's life and he treats the soldier-turned-teacher terribly. It is no wonder that Danny distrusts the Doctor. Danny sees the good in Clara, even as she lies to him to protect him, but he detests all the lying. Clara is, as Philip Purser-Hallard argues in *The Black Archive 4: Dark Water / Death in Heaven*, effectively unfaithful to him. Her behaviour blinds him from seeing the good that the Doctor brings to her life. However, as Simon Brew writes:

> '[W]hat makes this particularly work for me, and what makes it all the more heartbreaking, is that the relationship between Capaldi's Doctor and Clara has never been about romance. It's been about the Doctor needing Clara, and Clara wanting to be the Doctor. That they care for each other, they're both brilliant and lonely, and they both make each other better.'[33]

Then, in *Dark Water* (2014), Danny dies. He is run over. There is no purpose for it. No heroics. It is an entirely non-**Doctor Who** type of death, and Clara's reaction is at once ordinary grief and an extraordinary rage to fix it. This gets to the heart of Clara and the way she as a character bridges the idea of hero – of being the human lens through which we view the Doctor, and how most of us merely muddle through doing the best we can, which is what the Doctor

---

[33] Brew, Simon, '**Doctor Who** Series 9: *Face the Raven* Review'.

does despite all his pomposity, alien grandstanding and intelligence. Clara's grief for Danny permeates her subsequent actions all the way to her death in *Face the Raven*.

Clara is someone who 'enters', or at least tries to enter, the world or universe of their desire. She wants the adventure that travelling with the Doctor entails, as well as an ordinary relationship with an ordinary guy, Danny, who loves her; and, yet, there is an edge to Clara's behaviour all through the 2014 season that suggests a level of dissatisfaction. Rosalind Coward contends that 'Female dissatisfaction is constantly recast as desire,'[34] and Linda Hutcheon argues that women's pleasures are constructed; they are produced by discourses often sustaining men's privilege[35]. Most of the Doctor's companions are women who are often depicted as escaping their mundane lives in their TARDIS travels. Rose and Amy set precedents for the show in allowing the companion to simultaneously escape and remain at home in their domestic lives (albeit neither ultimately successfully). Clara, too, wants both the thrills of travelling with the Doctor and the stability of a relationship with Danny. Desire is Elspeth Probyn's point of departure in her essay 'Queer Belongings: the Politics of Departure'[36], and it is a concept that is not static. She says, 'we can recognize the ways in which desire points us not to a person, not to an individual, but to the movement of different body

---

[34] Coward, Rosalind, *Female Desire: Women's Sexuality Today*, p13.
[35] Hutcheon, Linda, *The Politics of Postmodernism*, p144.
[36] Probyn, Elspeth, 'Queer Belongings: The Politics of Departure' in Grosz, Elizabeth, and Elspeth Probyn, eds, *Sexy Bodies: The Strange Carnalities of Feminism*, p4

parts.'[37] More than that, for Probyn desire 'is not a metaphor, it is a method of doing things, of getting places.'[38] When one considers desire as something that is by definition unobtainable, then the motion — the constant departing and arriving — tied to desire becomes an important factor in understanding Clara's desires and how they lead ultimately to her death.

Concepts of desire have been explored throughout Western philosophical history. Psychoanalysis is one strand of thought that engages with the questions raised by desire; Elizabeth Grosz traces the history of psychoanalysis back to Plato via Hegel. She writes that 'for Hegel, the only object that both satisfies desire and perpetrates it is not an object but another desire. The desire of the other is thus the only appropriate object of desire.'[39] Clara wants to be the Doctor, who is very much 'the other', which is therefore impossible. Grosz states that the Freudian and Lacanian traditions saw desire as:

> 'the movement of substitution that creates a series of equivalent objects to fill this primordial lack [... This] endless chain is an effect of an oedipalising process that requires the child's relinquishing its incestual attachments with the creation of an endless network of replacements, substitutes, and representations of the perpetually absent object.'[40]

The 12th Doctor and Clara can be seen as simultaneously taking on

---

[37] Probyn, 'Queer Belongings', p14.
[38] Probyn, 'Queer Belongings', p2.
[39] Grosz, Elizabeth. *Space, Time and Perversion: Essays on the Politics of Bodies*, p176.
[40] Grosz, *Space, Time and Perversion*, p176.

a fatherly and motherly role to each other, both addressing a lack in the other. They save each other's lives on numerous occasions: Clara comforts the child who becomes the Doctor[41], and gives his adult self a set of cards to help his emotional response to others[42]. Grosz points out there are other concepts of desire that do not posit it in terms of lack. Spinoza, for example, argues that 'desire is the force of positive production, the action that creates things, makes alliances, and forges interactions'[43]. This is another way to see the Doctor and Clara's relationship, and that of Danny and Clara, and later Clara's with Ashildr at the end of time[44].

Clara is full of life and mischief and she throws herself into her triple life as a dedicated English teacher, travelling companion of the Doctor, and romantic partner to Danny. All of these three strands prove ultimately to be too much, particularly as two are complicated and incomplete, which is the tragedy of Clara during both the 2014 and 2015 seasons. Ordinarily, splitting a life between a full-time job as intense as teaching teenagers and a life-risking adventure with the Doctor would be enough to push the average human being to breaking point. Add into that mix a new, serious relationship and the ingredients for disaster are primed, especially because the Doctor is far from being a good role model and Danny is an astute judge of character. The emotional lies build and build between the Doctor, Clara and Danny, and frequently reach what should be a catharsis, only to be mostly ignored. They continue to build until Danny dies

---

[41] *Listen*.
[42] First seen in *Under the Lake* (2015).
[43] Grosz, *Space, Time and Perversion*, p179.
[44] *Hell Bent*.

and is resurrected as a Cyberman.

Clara tries to emulate the Doctor, but she is fundamentally different from him in behaviour as well as being. As Ohila of the Sisterhood of Karn says of the Doctor in *Hell Bent*, he always runs **away** from everything and everyone, and Clara runs **to** adventure and danger. Danny's death is just one more horror she has survived. In every story of her last season, Clara is a fully-fledged adventurer without any regard for the consequences. It's not that she is suicidal, just reckless because she has survived so much. She has been with the Doctor for so long and faced such danger, witnessed a lot of brutal deaths, she thinks she's invincible[45]. We see the tail-end of high-risk adventure at the start of *The Girl Who Died* (2015), and also during *Face the Raven* when she hangs from the open TARDIS door as they fly over London.

Kaitlin Thomas summarises Clara and the underlying motivations driving her in *Face the Raven*:

> 'Clara derived pleasure from escaping death, and it's likely that she'd have continued on this path of self-destruction until eventually it caught up to her. But why? [...] I think it's safe to say it's tied to the events of last season's finale [...] being with the Doctor was actually her way of dealing with the pain. I don't think Clara consciously wanted to die even as she walked toward her death — she was sad and she was scared — but she was trying to be brave the way Danny had been brave.'[46]

---

[45] **Doctor Who Extra** episode 10, *Face the Raven* DVD.
[46] Thomas, Kaitlin, '**Doctor Who** *Face the Raven* Review: Swan Song'.

The Tragedy of Clara Oswald

'She faces the Raven. She doesn't run from it. She is who she is right to the end.'

[Steven Moffat][47]

Once Danny is dead, Clara throws herself at life with the Doctor with reckless abandon. It is as though the complicated third part of her life has gone and, on the surface at least, is no matter. Jenna Coleman described the effect as forcing a change in perspective rather than a reaction to the death, or running away from her memories of Danny[48].

Clara has learned a set of lessons well from the Doctor and her experiences with him. She has pretty much vanquished any fear she may have had previously. We see this during *The Magician's Apprentice / The Witch's Familiar* (2015) in her role with Missy as a fall-guy in a lively double-act – though her fear isn't entirely gone. Clara's panic is real when Missy traps her inside the Dalek and Clara realises that she cannot communicate clearly to the Doctor. Yet, it is a momentary panic because the Doctor and her own pluckiness rescues her from a twist on the fate of Oswin Oswald.

In *Face the Raven,* all of what has been building finally reaches its climax. The story ties up all the threads of Clara believing she can be like the Doctor, that she can lie to help save others without endangering her own life, and that she is clever enough to play the

---

[47] **Doctor Who Extra** episode 10.
[48] 'Wil Wheaton Interviews Peter Capaldi and Jenna Coleman'. *Face the Raven* DVD.

games of which the Doctor is a master.

Clara shines when she tries to emulate the Doctor, most obviously in *Flatline* when the Doctor is trapped in the TARDIS. One of the lessons she learns with regards to the Doctor's special brand of leadership is that lying is not always a bad thing. In fact, lying to keep up people's hope in hopeless situations is good because of its effectiveness in saving them. Dan Martin observes that 'it was a canny move to bring back Rigsy for her [Clara's] exit[49]' because it enables the audience to remember Clara as the Doctor and Rigsy as her companion against the Boneless, which ultimately leads to the tragedy of *Face the Raven*. Danny, through his questions to Clara about the Doctor in *Flatline* and other stories, brings to the fore the Doctor's moral ambiguity. We, the audience, and she, Clara, are reminded frequently that the Doctor is alien. For all his heroism and championing of doing right, the Doctor's moral codes are not the same as what are broadly referred to as human, but really are Western values. In *Kill the Moon* (2014) Clara believes the Doctor has forced her to make a terrible decision. It is, of course, the sort of decision the Doctor is forced to make all the time in order to save as many lives as possible. However, we later see that Clara's ability to lie helps her survive the Zygons in *The Zygon Inversion* (2015). In this, she has clearly picked up some of the Doctor's moral ambiguity.

Clara's death is as brave as it is foolhardy and reckless. Her goal to save Rigsy's life is achieved, but her miscalculation about the Doctor and Mayor Ashildr's ability to save her from death creates her tragedy. It is precisely Clara's mistaken belief that she is capable of being the Doctor that makes her death in *Face the Raven* the most

---

[49] Martin, Dan, '**Doctor Who** Series 35, Episode 10: *Face the Raven*'.

literary type of tragedy. Here are echoes with Adric, with both characters arrogantly assuming their cleverness can save others just like the Doctor does, but death proves to be their comeuppance. Newspaper critic Jon Cooper was one who highlighted Clara's death as a punishment for her chutzpah:

> 'Clara's increasing recklessness had a big hand in her comeuppance – she dies because she assumes too much, that she knows much more than everyone else and, come what may, the Doctor will always be there to rescue her [...] Clara was too clever too half [sic] and she suffered for it.'[50]

However, **Doctor Who** is usually far more forgiving of its characters' fatal recklessness. The first Doctor summarised this misplaced sacrifice of his friends when he said of Katarina:

> 'She didn't understand. She couldn't understand. She wanted to save our lives. And perhaps the lives of all the other beings in the solar system. I hope she's found her perfection. We shall always remember her as one of the daughters of the gods.'[51]

The fifth Doctor, Tegan and Nyssa lament Adric's sacrifice, but because they did not witness his final, doomed attempt to be as clever as the Doctor, the show doesn't bring to the surface the question of his death being his comeuppance for his arrogance. The text of the show makes it clear that his sacrifice was noble.

In *Face the Raven*, the Doctor's rage at Clara's impending death from

---

[50] Cooper, Jon, '**Doctor Who**: *Face the Raven*, TV Review – Fans Left Reeling by Shock Ending to Gothic Emotional Rollercoaster'.
[51] 'The Traitors' (*The Daleks' Master Plan*, 1966).

her own recklessness is directed towards Ashildr, which Clara herself tries to redirect. The rage and grief we see the Doctor express in this and in *Heaven Sent* and *Hell Bent* opens up various readings of Clara's tragedy.

The idea of it being in some way a punishment for her desire to be the 12th Doctor, or at least be as much like him as she can, is something that numerous critics of *Face the Raven* note. Rob Smedley describes Clara as cocky and states that 'Hubris is her downfall [...] And unlike the Doctor, she has to face up to the consequences of what she's done.'[52] Ree Hines describes it as 'Clara 101, which is to say: well-meaning, but completely reckless and a bit arrogant. She doesn't just want to act like the Doctor; she seems to think she is the Doctor. Or at least as capable.'[53] Simon Brew ascribes her building cockiness and acting like the Doctor as being the reason for her death: 'One day, she was always going to overreach. And that day was today.'[54]

While other critics place Clara's desire to be as much like the Doctor as possible at the root of her misplaced sacrifice in *Face the Raven*, they see the outcome more as foolishness than punishment. Rob Smedley observes that 'playing at being the Doctor gets you killed. Of course it does. It even gets the Doctor killed now and then[55].' Kaitlin Thomas, too, points to how Clara's recklessness and stupidity

---

[52] Smedley, Rob, '**Doctor Who** Season 9 Episode 10 Review: *Face the Raven*'.
[53] Hines, Ree, '**Doctor Who** Recap Season 9, Episode 10, *Face The Raven*: Clara Oswald's Finest Hour Is Her Last'.
[54] Brew, '*Face the Raven* Review'.
[55] Smedley, '*Face the Raven*'.

is very like the Doctor's behaviour, but:

> 'Clara is not the Doctor, and no matter how hard she tried to emulate him this season, she was never going to be the Doctor. In all of time and space there can be only one and even the Doctor has days in which he struggles to be that man'.[56]

Emily Asher-Perrin pinpoints how *Face the Raven* portrays the Clara-Doctor relationship, both as characters and in how **Doctor Who** portrays sacrifice and death:

> 'Clara was in it for the danger, for the mystery, for the ability to be hero. She got her wish. It doesn't seem like a punishment for her choices, merely a logical outcome, one that she accepts because she's always known it was coming. It is a logical outcome for the Doctor as well – the only difference for him is that he is, as he put it, slightly less breakable.'[57]

The creators behind the 12th Doctor and Clara, both over the arc of their story and in *Face the Raven,* specifically point to how Clara's death is a logical consequence of who she is and her recklessness and love of adventure. Steven Moffat emphasises that Clara is a thrill-seeker who runs as close to the edge as she can, and with the Doctor and Ashildr there she thinks she's not really going to die[58].

---

[56] Thomas, 'Swan Song'.
[57] Asher-Perrin, Emily, 'Let Me Be Brave: **Doctor Who** – *Face the Raven'*.
[58] **Doctor Who Extra** episode 10.

Sarah Dollard says:

> 'She's having fun. She's not of a suicidal bent. She's swept up in the adventure. High on the adrenaline. It's not a death drive. She's not thinking of consequences.'[59]

Asher-Perrin points out that 'For all that Clara Oswald was on the TARDIS to fulfil her own desire for adventure and excitement [...] she takes care of the people who matter to her.'[60] In *Face the Raven*, Clara makes the ultimate sacrifice in order to protect her friend Rigsy, but it is not the first time the character has died for others. Previous versions of the character sacrificed themselves in *Asylum of the Daleks* and *The Snowmen*, both of which were the result of her first ultimate sacrifice during *The Name of the Doctor*, when she runs into the Doctor's time stream and is fractured across time and space throughout the Doctor's life. In this, she again shows how paradoxically she is like the Doctor in risking the few (even him or herself) to save the many, but not in that she runs towards danger rather than having her heroism forced upon her, as the Doctor often does.

Clara is ultimately, in life and death, simultaneously both ordinary and extraordinary. Her name is apt, coming from the feminine form of the Latin 'clarus', meaning bright. Clara does indeed shine brightly for two Doctors – three if you include John Hurt's War Doctor. 'Oswin' and 'Oswald' are Old English names sharing a root, and – echoing the role Clara plays in pushing the way gender is discussed in **Doctor**

---

[59] Dollard, Sarah, live commentary on *Face the Raven*, at Gallifrey One convention, 12 February 2016.
[60] Asher-Perrin, 'Let Me Be Brave'.

Who[61] – are boys' names. 'Oswald' means 'God's power', while Oswin means 'God's friend'. If the Doctor can be seen as a surrogate for a god[62], then Clara's last name is significant. Further, the Old English 'Os' is cognate with the Old Norse 'As' meaning that Ashildr's name shares this root with Clara's names. Ashildr means 'battle of the gods'; these names underline the dynamic between both women in their relationship with each other and with the Doctor.

---

[61] Seen mostly by the consistent misgendering of her by Strax.

[62] Groenewegen, Sarah, 'Don't Tell the Sisterhood' in Burk, Graeme, and Robert Smith?, eds, *Time Unincorporated Volume 2*, pp334-39.

CHAPTER 2: REPERCUSSIONS

'Every great decision creates ripples, like a huge boulder dropped in a lake. The ripples merge, rebound off the banks in unforeseeable ways. The heavier the decision, the larger the waves, the more uncertain the consequences.'

[The Doctor, *Remembrance of the Daleks* episode 2 (1988)]

The Doctor seems to see everything in terms of patterns, with connections made across time and space, sometimes beyond. This ability has grown more sophisticated as the character and series have grown older. The seventh Doctor, both in his television stories and in the extended oeuvre of the Virgin Publishing **New Adventures** novels (1991-97), is the master strategist and chess-player with the gods or godlike, and with a commanding view across history. His role of 'Time's Champion' is picked up through all the hints and explicit storytelling about the Time War and the Doctor's part in it. The 10th, 11th and 12th Doctors all wrestle with the conflict their role as hero generates, their decisions weighing heavily on them and rippling out to affect their companions and enemies.

Yet the Doctor appears quite blind to the full range of repercussions in almost all of his actions. The character might see where logic would dictate the likeliest of reactions to certain actions, but the Doctor often fails to consider the range of emotional responses and the role of irrationality in human decision-making. The 12th Doctor did not see the decisions that led Clara to make her plan to save Rigsy in *Face the Raven*, leading him to blame Ashildr the Mayor[63]. It is

---

[63] While Ashildr adopts the name 'Me' in *The Woman Who Lived*, the

clear that, while he thinks he knows what truly drives Ashildr, that view is questionable.

The theme of recklessness and its consequences ripples beyond the actions of Clara in *Face the Raven*, as do the questions about the meaning of death, resurrection and immortality in a time-travel show like **Doctor Who**. Ashildr is the living example of someone who died, but is resurrected as an immortal by the Doctor with consequences that rebound against others in unexpected ways.

This chapter explores the role of Ashildr in the tragedy of Clara Oswald, and the broader ways in which Ashildr poses questions about the archetypal villains in **Doctor Who**. It also looks at the other returning character, Rigsy.

Ashildr's Return

'Infinite lifespan, finite memory – it makes for an awkward social life.'

[Ashildr]

Doctor Who, as action-adventure, often glosses over the marks inevitably left by travelling around as much as the Doctor has, and meeting as many people and creatures as he does. Occasionally those marks, for good or evil, are seen by the audience and by the Doctor. The two Peladon television stories[64] are rare in that we see a non-Earth locale which the Doctor visits twice, and the people there remember him. He has become a legend, a friend. Then in *Timelash*

---

scripts for *Face the Raven* and *Hell Bent* use 'Ashildr'. I default to that name, too, unless otherwise noted for specificity.
[64] *The Curse of Peladon* (1972) and *The Monster of Peladon* (1974).

(1985) there are references to the Doctor having visited Karfel before, which is remembered by the inhabitants. However, as Gary Russell asks, 'does the Doctor always get it right? In his efforts to save the smaller picture, is it possible that occasionally the bigger picture, the Web of Time itself, can be broken by his actions?'[65]

The most famous questioning of consequences in **Doctor Who**'s history is from *Genesis of the Daleks* (1975) when the Doctor says:

> 'If someone who knew the future pointed out a child to you and told you that that child would grow up totally evil, to be a ruthless dictator who would destroy millions of lives... could you then kill that child?'[66]

The choice then is taken from the Doctor, the incubating mutants survive, allowing Davros to fulfil his plans for the Daleks, and the Daleks (often with or against Davros) wreak havoc across the universe. The Doctor regrets not being able to make the choice to destroy the Daleks before they really started, although the character rationalises that for all the grief the Daleks have brought, they have also brought good through bringing together people to fight them and survive them. The show re-questions the Doctor's dilemma about destroying the Daleks before they begin in *The Magician's Apprentice / The Witch's Familiar* when the Doctor faces the choice to save the boy Davros or let him die.

---

[65] Russell, Gary, *Short Trips: Repercussions* (2004), cover blurb. The collection of short stories is bounded by a narrative exploring the unintended consequences of the Doctor's interventions in people's lives.

[66] *Genesis of the Daleks* episode 6.

The Daleks, with or without Davros, are far from the only foes to return more than once to battle the Doctor. That pantheon has grown over the decades, and when some are selected to return, the stories play on and into the similar-yet-different theme of **Doctor Who**. The Sontarans, for example, have changed over time from warriors indifferent to their effect on history[67], to sadistic torturers[68], to friends whose intrinsic warlike nature is played for its comedy value[69].

Storytelling, too, has returned periodically to overarching plots — the Key to Time[70], Bad Wolf[71], Mr Saxon[72], the Impossible Girl[73] — but most stories are, broadly speaking, standalone. The 2015 season of **Doctor Who** did something new. It introduced Ashildr, who appeared in four stories, each by a different writer[74]. *The Girl Who Died* and *The Woman Who Lived* (2015) follow each other, but the latter is not the usual second part to an ongoing **Doctor Who** story. Rather than resolving a cliffhanger, or continuing an adventure, the second of these two stories is almost entirely about the new character's narrative arc, focussing on the repercussions of the

---

[67] *The Time Warrior* (1973-4).

[68] *The Sontaran Experiment* (1975).

[69] Commander Strax in *A Good Man Goes to War* (2011), *The Snowmen, The Crimson Horror, The Name of the Doctor, Deep Breath* (2014) and various mini-episodes, short stories and comic strips.

[70] 1978-79.

[71] 2005.

[72] 2007.

[73] 2012-13.

[74] *The Girl Who Died* by Jamie Mathieson and Steven Moffat, *The Woman Who Lived* (2015) by Catherine Tregenna, *Face the Raven* by Sarah Dollard, and *Hell Bent* by Steven Moffat.

Doctor's actions in saving Ashildr and making her immortal. *The Woman Who Lived* sees the Doctor on his own in England during 1651 attempting to find an artefact, but he finds Ashildr as a Lady moonlighting as a highwayman for thrills. Most of the story unpicks Ashildr's problems as an immortal with a poor memory, her pain at having children and losing them to plague, and her recklessness in both her thrill-seeking and her naive alliance with the alien Leandro.

The Doctor's actions in returning Ashildr from death and making her immortal are unusual. Usually, the Doctor vehemently refuses to interfere to change significant events such as the deaths of friends. In terms of the production, this consistent refusal ensures that the show resists the trap of using time travel as a way to cheat. The erratic nature of the TARDIS, whether as a creature with its own sentience or as piloted by the Doctor, is the key plot device that drives the adventure narrative. Yet, with Ashildr the Doctor goes against almost everything he has ever done in the past, which prompts questions as to why. When the Doctor, Clara and the villagers discover Ashildr has died just as the Vikings heroically see off the Mire, we see the Doctor remember Donna Noble demanding that at least one person should survive the eruption of Vesuvius[75]. Perhaps, then, he sees something else in Ashildr that he doesn't articulate to anyone else. The Doctor tries to be kind to Ashildr in leaving a second chip for her to give to a person with whom she decides she would like to live with for rest of eternity; but this option is closed off in *The Woman Who Lived*.

Jamie Mathieson says that the character was always going to be a

---

[75] In *The Fires of Pompeii* (2008).

Viking made immortal by the Doctor, but her part grew once the young actor Maisie Williams, best known for her role in **Game of Thrones** (2011-), was cast[76]. Ashildr is clearly one of a kind amongst the Vikings the Doctor and Clara meet entirely by chance. The Viking girl believes she has premonitions, and is a creative story-teller. She is loved by her village and she in turns loves her village, and yet she is an outsider. Her father, Einarr (who the Doctor renames 'Chuckles'), tells her that she always thinks she is the one who brings bad luck.

After three stories with no mention of Ashildr, she returns and is revealed to be behind the trap set in *Face the Raven* to ensnare the Doctor. As Jon Cooper writes, 'Mayor Me's appearance is a direct consequence of the Doctor's meddling in the past, and so Clara's death can logically (though not wholly) be attributed to him.'[77]

The role of women in the writing team for **Doctor Who** is worth considering when thinking about the complexity of Ashildr as a recurring character who shifts from friend, to enemy, to something not quite either but whose life is intrinsically linked to Clara's fate. Feminist media theorists have studied the gender make-up of the writers and directors and the effects on women characters in sitcoms and dramas. Martha M Lauzen concluded in her study that:

> 'Women working behind the scenes give female characters more to say, let them introduce topics of conversation, and have the last word. In addition, female characters on shows

---

[76] Mathieson, Jamie, interviewed by Gary Russell at Gallifrey One convention, 12 February 2016.
[77] Cooper, 'Fans Left Reeling'.

where women are in charge interrupt and advise other characters more often'[78].

In *The Girl Who Died*, even though the story focusses on Ashildr, she is one of a relatively large ensemble cast engaged in an action-adventure story where we see glimpses of who she is. *The Woman Who Lived*, in contrast, almost entirely focusses on her as a character dealing with the repercussions of the Doctor's actions in her life, but with moments of action-adventure to punctuate what is mostly a dialogue between her and the Doctor.

The way **Doctor Who** is produced has changed over the decades, but some tenets have remained constant. Its first producer was a woman, Verity Lambert, and although much of the story and character development had been finalised before she took on the position, she wanted some focus on relationships so the new show would not be purely 'action-adventure'[79]. This is seen in the evolving dynamics between the Doctor, Susan, Ian and Barbara, and subsequently in each permutation of the Doctor and companions. The production of **Doctor Who** is a team effort, and because of its longevity, as Tulloch and Alvarado observed, 'incoming producers make judgements as to which audience groups they feel the programme is under-serving when they are considering what their own particular "signature" will be'[80]. However, while women have always been part of the show's various production teams, of the 826

---

[78] Lauzen, Martha M, 'Sisters of the Sitcoms', *Television Quarterly* vol 28 #4 (1997), p84.

[79] Lambert, Verity, interviewed in *More Than 30 Years in the TARDIS*, BBC Video, 1993.

[80] Tulloch and Alvarado, *The Unfolding Text*, p57.

episodes of the series made from 1963 to 2016, only 2.72% were written by women[81]. When the British press ran stories in 2014 about Neil Gaiman on Tumblr pointing to the fact that the series produced since 2008 had done nothing to address this statistic[82], the production team questioned their approach and two women were commissioned to write stories for the 2015 season, Catherine Tregenna (*The Woman Who Lived*) and Sarah Dollard (*Face the Raven*) – both featuring Ashildr as a fascinating antagonist for the Doctor[83].

Dollard's original storyline for *Face the Raven* did not have Ashildr in it. Instead, it featured a woman acting as a mayor of a trap street refugee camp in central London. Through the process of developing the story, the production team decided that Ashildr should return in this story and take up the mayoral role, thereby linking the story directly into various narrative arcs to accentuate the similarities and differences between the Doctor, Clara, and Ashildr. According to Dollard, that single change of character did not cause her as a writer much extra work[84].

---

[81] Guerrier et al, *Whographica*, pp202-203. The full list of women credited as writing episodes or stories of **Doctor Who** to date is: Jane Baker, Barbara Clegg, Sarah Dollard, Paula Moore, Rona Munro, Helen Raynor, Lesley Scott and Catherine Tregenna.
[82] See for example, Hawkes, Rebecca, 'Why Are There No Female Writers on **Doctor Who**?', *The Daily Telegraph*, 9 October 2014.
[83] Dollard and Munro would both return for the 2017 season (with *Thin Ice* and *The Eaters of Light*), in the latter's case after nearly three decades' absence.
[84] Dollard, Gallifrey One live commentary.

Ashildr's Immortality

'I saved you. I didn't know your heart would rust because I kept it beating. I didn't think your conscience would need renewing, that the well of human kindness would run dry. I just wanted to save a terrified young woman's life.'

[The Doctor, *The Woman Who Lived*]

Ashildr is one of those characters introduced during Steven Moffat's tenure as showrunner where perception is everything, yet she hides a greater complexity. Moffat shows his cleverness in playing with the show's narrative structure in ways few have before. River Song is the most obvious other example of perception leading to interesting narratives; but unlike with River Song, the effect with Ashildr is far from explicit. With River, we first meet her just before her death but also before the Doctor has met her[85], and for some time each meeting tracks their relationship across time with one in reverse to the other, until the Doctor knows her well but she doesn't know him[86]. From the audience's perspective, which is the same as the Doctor's, River's life is shown mostly in reverse. The characters point this out at every opportunity, and it is usually a plot point in these stories.

As the Doctor's travelling companion, Clara's life is shown in all its

---

[85] *Silence in the Library / Forest of the Dead* (2008).
[86] Culminating in *Let's Kill Hitler* (2011), where she first takes on both Alex Kingston's form and the name 'River Song'. Her subsequent appearances have inevitably been set later in the character's timeline.

intensity over four years and during 36 television episodes[87]. We know that she has barely any time to recover from the building physical and emotional stress, and she goes through a lot of both. We know she has very little normal time, which for all she plainly enjoys the adventure is one of the major strains on her relationship with Danny. But, because we see almost all of this intensity, we perceive that there is more there than there actually is; this is a fairly common cognitive bias known as Availability Bias where we recall the unusual or remarkable quickly in a way that skews our perception of risk[88]. The way the television stories are told helps establish and build the ordinary/extraordinary dichotomous puzzle about her character.

In contrast, Ashildr's life plods on from when the Doctor makes her immortal during the eighth century through to the end of time. In the television series[89], we see her in sequential chronological order from her childhood through to her physically arrested young adulthood in 1651, then contemporary London, and finally we skip to the end of time where she waits and is found by the Doctor. We only have her words to describe what she has done during that time, either spoken or written down, and because most of her conversations are with the Doctor the scant slivers we see are cast

---

[87] Counting the fragments of her persona who appear in *Asylum of the Daleks* and *The Snowmen*, but not her brief postmortem cameo in *Twice Upon a Time* (2017).

[88] Kahneman, Daniel. *Thinking Fast and Slow*, chapters 12 and 13; Dobilli, Rolf, *The Art of Thinking Clearly*, pp35-37.

[89] While she does appear in the BBC Books-Penguin collection of stories *The Legends of Ashildr* (2015), I only refer to the television stories.

through that light. Clara tells us in *Face the Raven,* via conversation with Ashildr the Mayor, that the Doctor has got 'this whole secret room in the TARDIS where he collects mentions of' her, which he thinks Clara doesn't know about. However, we, the audience, perceive only a miniscule fraction of what is an incredibly long life.

Time in **Doctor Who** is most often depicted as linear, and it fits Henri Bergson's observation that 'when we speak of time, we generally think of a homogenous medium in which our conscious states are ranged alongside one another as in space.'[90] The reason time is linear in the textual diegesis of **Doctor Who** lies with the narrative structure employed by the producers. Anne Cranny-Francis notes that the quest narrative is the form that most science fiction takes. Usually, the temporal sequencing is linear, especially in the popular science fiction of film (particularly Hollywood blockbusters) and television series. Narrative plotting is one of the major semiotic practices of our society, since it is easier to read the intended meaning. It is easier because to all intents and purposes it is invisible to us, because of how we see time[91]. Margery Hourihan, who discusses **Doctor Who** in relation to her work on the hero in children's literature, supports this argument:

> 'In hero tales [...] the story takes the form of a journey and the sense of linear progression is strong. These stories are exciting and easy to read. They create pleasure by arousing [...] the

---

[90] Bergson, Henri, *Time and Free Will: An Essay on the Immediate Data of Consciousness*, p90.

[91] Cranny-Francis, Anne, *Feminist Fiction: Feminist Uses of Generic Fiction*, pp10–11.

desire to know "what will happen next". As each incident in the story concludes the desire is temporarily satisfied, only to be restimulated as the hero moves on to the next challenge.'[92]

This sequencing technique is particularly prevalent in science fiction film and television to allow the fantastic tales to be explored without losing the casual audience. This includes **Doctor Who** in the majority of its run. Moffat is an exception in that he confidently plays with time as a plot device in numerous of his stories as individual writer and in arcs under his tenure as showrunner. More often, **Doctor Who** accords with Patricia S Warrick's argument about science fiction stories using certain signifiers to illustrate dislocation from the present[93].

Western philosophy binds time and space together as concepts, just as they are both bound to questions of being and consciousness. Martin Heidegger, borrowing from Liebniz, says that 'time is constitutive of space'[94]. Bergson argued that 'if time, as immediate consciousness perceives it, were, like space, a homogenous medium, science would be able to deal with it, as it can with space.'[95] Grosz observed that:

> 'Newtonian mechanics [...] reduces temporal relations to spatial form insofar as the temporal relations between events

---

[92] Hourihan, *Deconstructing the Hero*, p46.
[93] Warrick, Patricia S, *The Cybernetic Imagination in Science Fiction*, pp82–83.
[94] Heidegger, Martin, *History of the Concept of Time: Prolegomena*, p234.
[95] Bergson, *Time and Free Will*, p234.

are represented by the relations between points on a straight line. Even today the equation of temporal relations with the continuum of numbers assumes that time is isomorphic with space, and that space and time exist as a continuum, a unified totality. Time is capable of representation only through its subordination to space and spatial models.'[96]

Doctor Who rarely questions the general Western conceptions of time and space. It fits neatly with the still dominant conception of Newtonian mechanics. Ashildr's story arc is precisely this conception, which contrasts with the ways in which Moffat plays repeatedly with time in his story-telling in **Doctor Who**.

Eleanore Kofman and Elizabeth Lebas argue Lefebvre's point that 'History has to be understood as praxis which is the production of people by people.'[97] In science fiction, this becomes obvious and even extended as the projected futures are also the production of people in the here and now. Warrick observes that science fiction time travel stories arose shortly after Darwin's theories of evolution became popularly known. She argues that much of the way time is presented in science fiction is evolutionary in nature[98]. Rules govern how time is portrayed in **Doctor Who**, and most of these rules firmly locate time as a linear, teleological sequence of events within each serial or story[99]. As Hourihan says, the 'idea of time as an irreversible

[96] Grosz, *Space, Time and Perversion*, p95.
[97] Kofman, Eleanore, and Elizabeth Lebas, *Henri Lefebvre: Writings on Cities*, p18.
[98] Warrick, *The Cybernetic Imagination in Science Fiction*, p106.
[99] Nearly all of **Doctor Who** between 1963 and 1989 was shown as a series of multi-episode serials, but from 2005 mostly as single or

sequence of moments has become the normal view of most educated Westerners and is, Gould argues, an essential basis for the treatment of history as intelligible.'[100] It is this view of history and time that is prevalent in **Doctor Who**, even as Moffat plays with River Song's timeline.

However, the Doctor's personal relationship with time has changed over the life of the series. **Doctor Who** is a series that is approaching its sixth decade and there have been shifts in science fiction conceptions of time. At first, time in **Doctor Who** was familiar from the concept as explored in HG Wells: time was something that could be manipulated by eccentric scientists. Peter Osborne notes that scheduling became a vital part of everyday life with the rise of capitalism[101]. The desire to circumvent such rigorous scheduling became a standard theme in early science fiction tales, tied as they were to capitalism. It was no accident, for example, that the third Doctor continually sought to overcome the strictures of his exile to late 20th-century England by trying to regain the secrets of time travel: that is, to regain the freedom to be a renegade, to escape. As **Doctor Who** continued, there was exploration of the idea that a Time Lord could have a symbiotic relationship with time. Gilles Deleuze's description of time and history is pertinent to the way both are usually depicted in **Doctor Who**:

'We place ourselves at once in the past; we leap into the past as into a proper element. In the same way that we do not

double-episode stories, occasionally as triple-episode stories.
[100] Hourihan, *Deconstructing the Hero*, p45.
[101] Osborne, Peter, 'The Politics of Time', *Radical Philosophy* #68, 1994, p5.

perceive things in ourselves, but at the place where they are, we only grasp the past at the place where it is in itself, and not in ourselves, in our present. There is therefore a "past in general" that is not the particular past of a particular present but that is like an ontological element, a past that is eternal and for all time, the condition of the "passage" of every particular present.'[102]

We do not see many of the events that shape Ashildr's course through her ages-long life as we do those of Clara's considerably shorter life[103]. We are told about Ashildr's grief at losing her children when the Doctor reads some of her journals, but we do not witness it as we witness Clara's grief at losing Danny. We know the Doctor keeps an eye on Ashildr throughout time only because Clara tells us he does. Once Ashildr becomes immortal we only see three chapters of her incredibly long life when it intersects directly with the Doctor: her life in 1651 as a Lady and highwaywoman, then as self-proclaimed Mayor of the trap street in contemporary London, and finally at the end of the universe.

At the end of the universe, when she is the last immortal left, Ashildr questions the Doctor's morals in wanting to extend Clara's life by taking her memories of him away from her. The Doctor protests that he is doing so to protect Clara from the Time Lords, but as first Ashildr and then Clara herself says, there is no point for her in living without those memories. Those memories have made her who she is. This echoes back once more to Donna Noble, condemned to live with no

---

[102] Deleuze, Gilles, *Bergsonism*, p56.
[103] At least up to *Hell Bent,* when she joins Ashildr in a TARDIS in the moment before her heart stops.

memory of the Doctor and her time with him; Donna being who the Doctor remembers when he decides to revive Ashildr and make her immortal. Memory and its loss are important for Ashildr, of course, because by 1651 – a relatively short time from when the Doctor made her immortal, when compared with the sum of her entire life – she had forgotten more than she had ever known.

Not Your Typical Doctor Who Villain

ASHILDR

I don't pretend it's selfless. Being useful to them is useful to me. I need an anchor. A purpose. I think the Doctor might understand a little about that.

[…]

TO THE DOCTOR

It took me a long time to accept it. But you and I? We're the same.

['Trap Street: Purple Script'][104]

Ashildr is first portrayed as a particular type of familiar **Doctor Who** character; a bit of an outsider, a bit nerdy, an unlikely hero, but brave and unselfish when the need demands it. If Ashildr wasn't loved by her village, she would probably be an outsider. She is an oddity, as her father observes she thinks she is responsible for any misfortune that befalls their village. She is intelligent, and there are clues that

---

[104] Dollard, Sarah, '**Doctor Who** Series 9 Episode 10 "Trap Street": Purple Script', p26. 'Trap Street' was the working title for *Face the Raven* until at least 22 June 2015.

she is what we would now call genderqueer: not entirely a girl, and not entirely a boy. Maisie Williams is well cast as Ashildr. The role that made her name, Arya Stark in **Game of Thrones**, is also a girl who acts boyishly even before circumstances force her to pretend to be a boy.

Gender and sexual deviancy have been codes for the monstrous for decades of popular Western culture, which plays out in some interesting ways with Ashildr. Z Isiling Nataf describes how certain audiences from minority groups have a disrupted view of what they are watching:

> 'Something appears strange or amiss such that the film's authority, truth and accuracy are all challenged. Its ideological system shows through and disrupts identification and the natural flow of the narrative. These spectators [of 'deviant' sexuality and/or gender] are simultaneously hailed to engage with the film and are distanced by it. From this position of wary detachment, the spectator can read against the grain or intentions of the film-maker and identify with the villains in the narrative, for example, because they are shown disrupting the social order.'[105]

At least until the villains are vanquished, as she further notes.

Ashildr as the Knightmare dons the disguise of a highwayman because it is effective, but while there was real historical precedent her cross-dressing is still transgressive. During 1651 several key

---

[105] Isiling Nataf, Z, 'Black Lesbian Spectatorship and Pleasure in Popular Cinema' in Berston, Paul and Colin Richardson, eds, *A Queer Romance: Lesbians, Gay Men and Popular Culture*, p59.

events and battles of the English Civil War ravaged the country, including the escape of Charles II to France. There was at least one highwaywoman believed to be active during the time of the fictional Knightmare; the notoriety of Catherine Ferrers (1634–60) has survived to today, but there are questions about how true the allegations of her robbing were[106]. The historical record is more certain about women active as pirates in the English colonies in the Caribbean and the Americas at the same time. Women pirates often disguised themselves as men to circumvent the male-dominated codes of piracy. In *The Woman Who Lived*, Ashildr as Lady Me is meant to be regarded as having turned evil from her bitterness at what the Doctor did to her, with the Doctor forcing her to see her wicked ways to redeem them. Maisie Williams says that by *Face the Raven* her character is no longer evil, but does disrupt the Doctor's world[107]. Indeed, as Dan Martin describes:

'The Doctor knows he is responsible for the creation of this person, but he's powerless to stop her going down the routes he doesn't approve of. And after her stint as a 17th-century highwaywoman, reigning mischief over all she surveyed, her maturity 400 years later has led her to the exact same God complex that led to him creating her in the first place – taking her sense of responsibility to murderous levels.'[108]

Her name when translated as 'battle of the gods' takes on an interesting layer of meaning here, even more so with knowledge of the events in *Hell Bent*.

---

[106] White, Barbara, 'Ferrers, Catherine (1634–1660)'.
[107] **Doctor Who Extra** episode 10.
[108] Martin, '*Face the Raven*'.

Ashildr is not only transgressive in her cross-dressing. In each story that she appears in after *The Girl Who Died* there are indications that Ashildr is attracted to Clara. When they meet in *Face the Raven* Ashildr tells Clara that she is 'as beautiful as your photos.' Ashildr always asks the Doctor about Clara and his relationship with her in a way that is not necessarily restricted to her desire to understand the Doctor's motivations and triggers. Sarah Dollard has pointed out that Clara and the Mayor flirt quite a bit with each other[109].

Yvonne Tasker notes that the 'extratextual rumour' of queerness can attract queer interaction with the text[110]. Clare Whatling elaborates on this concept by suggesting 'that knowing that a particular actress is rumoured to be lesbian makes possible an appropriation of her films as lesbian texts, regardless of the possibilities the films themselves offer.'[111] Tasker and Whatling's observations can be extended to the writers and other creative members of a production. Sarah Dollard is openly queer and on social media often discusses gender and gender performance[112]. She included a whole scene where Clara and Anahson (who is forced to pose as a boy for her survival) explore issues of gender and performance, but this was cut before shooting began on the story[113]. She also revisited the suggestion first made in *The Magician's Apprentice* that Clara has kissed Jane Austen. The overtness of Clara's bisexuality, plus the

---

[109] Dollard, Gallifrey One live commentary.
[110] Tasker, Yvonne, *Working Girls: Gender and Sexuality in Popular Cinema*, p23.
[111] Whatling, Clare, *Screen Dreams*, p145.
[112] Sarah Dollard's @snazdoll Twitter account, Tumblr posts.
[113] Dollard, Gallifrey One live commentary.

inclusion of overtly same-sex relationships with Vastra and Jenny[114], and later Bill Potts and Heather[115], disrupts the 'queer as villain' motif and leads to nuance in characters like Ashildr.

Ashildr is not a typical **Doctor Who** monster or villain. Sarah Dollard says that it was vitally important for her story that Ashildr as the Mayor truly believes she is doing the right thing. She describes Ashildr in *Face the Raven* as hardened and doing the opposite of what she sees as the Doctor's faults, which ironically makes her weak in ways that the Time Lords can exploit[116]. Peter Capaldi observes that while the character is older and wiser by *Face the Raven*, she is being manipulated[117]. That manipulation points to the idea that Ashildr as the Mayor is far from being in as much control as she thinks she is, yet the uncontrollability of both her and the other pawns in the game played by those not even seen in this story means that the ripples bounce off in wholly unpredictable ways. The BBC website describes Ashildr's tragedy in *Face the Raven* thus:

> 'When Clara's attempt to protect Rigsy lead to her death, Ashildr is devastated. Her ruse to draw the Doctor onto the street is exposed, as is the fragility of her plan... She may have succeeded in trapping the Doctor, but in underestimating the lengths to which Clara would go for a friend, she ultimately sentenced her to death.'[118]

---

[114] *A Good Man Goes to War, The Snowmen, The Crimson Terror, The Name of the Doctor, Deep Breath.*
[115] *The Pilot, The Doctor Falls* (2017).
[116] Dollard, Gallifrey One live commentary.
[117] **Doctor Who Extra** episode 10.
[118] 'Ashildr', BBC **Doctor Who** site.

Prior to *Face the Raven*, and for all the Doctor lectures Ashildr about people and the need to care for them, she proves that she does care for them. Even as she tries to distance herself from people in general to avoid emotional entanglement and pain, she is not heartless. Her servant in *The Woman Who Lived* is someone who will not witness her agelessness. No doubt she has calculated that will protect her, but Ashildr also has a desire to not hurt him. She decides to become the person who will protect people against the Doctor. She does not want him as an enemy. Not because she fears him – after all, what else could he do to her beyond what he already has? – but because she wants to travel with him.

Her ambition is to keep her refugees safe in the bolt hole she rules in central London. Those refugees include individual examples of those very monsters the Doctor has fought and defeated over the centuries, but they are now trapped. These monsters are literally humanised with the technology that masks their true forms. That theme echoes the humanised Zygons and their fragile peace on Earth in *The Zygon Invasion / The Zygon Inversion* (2015).

The Return of Rigsy

DOCTOR

There's no nice way to say you're about to die.

RIGSY

What?!

DOCTOR

Rigsy...

RIGSY

No, no, no, no, no! Don't start using my actual name now. Call me pudding-brain. Call me local knowledge, whatever. Just don't call me Rigsy. You're going to save me. You're a Doctor. That's what you do.

Ashildr is not the only character to make a return appearance in *Face the Raven*, aside from the Doctor and Clara. One of the characters in *Flatline*, Rigsy, gets into trouble and calls Clara via the Doctor. As explored in the previous chapter, *Flatline* saw Clara taking on the role of the Doctor, receiving advice from within the shrunken TARDIS but still finding herself having issues getting through to the endangered people.

Step up Rigsy, a young artist on a community service programme in Bristol because of his graffiti, who helps Clara when others on his crew are reluctant. His decency and bravery strike a chord with Clara and later the Doctor, and they all become friends. It makes sense that Clara would give the young man a contact number for emergencies. Perhaps he reminds her a bit of Danny Pink, who is in London while they are in Bristol. Or perhaps she sees a potential uncomplicated relationship with Rigsy; a counterpoint to her complicated relationships with both Danny and the Doctor at the time of *Flatline*. (Clara is caught in a tangle of lies with Danny at this time, having told him she had given up her adventures with the Doctor when, obviously, she has not.)

There are similarities between Rigsy in *Flatline* and Ashildr in *The Girl Who Died*. Both are young. Both are brave and a little foolhardy. Both are creative, which puts them at odds with the society in which they live. They both become instant friends with Clara, and with both it takes the Doctor a little bit of time to see their greater qualities.

For all the two share similarities, Rigsy and Ashildr are also very different. While Rigsy puts himself in harm's way to save the world from the Boneless, he does not die. Despite his two encounters with impossible monsters and aliens, Rigsy remains in contemporary England and as much as he pushes societal boundaries he lives within them. He also doesn't desire to travel with the Doctor.

There is another crucial difference that Emily Asher-Perrin notes in her review of *Face the Raven*:

> 'There are a number of topical aspects to this episode that look very different when examined without the sheen of aliens and time travel, and the idea of framing a black man for murder to appease a tense community cannot be ignored in this context.'[119]

The other topical aspect of the story that Asher-Perrin refers to is the refugee community in hiding in contemporary London, which is the subject of the next chapter.

---

[119] Asher-Perrin, 'Let Me Be Brave'.

CHAPTER 3: LONDON

'Anyone who thinks that trap streets belong in **Doctor Who** gets **Doctor Who**.'

[Steven Moffat, **Writing Who**]

Earth is an important space for **Doctor Who**. Even though the textual diegesis of the series is such that the Doctor could go anywhere and to any time, the majority of the stories are set in familiar places in the south of England in times that are mostly contemporary. Because many of the companions are from also from contemporary England, this allows for playing up the contrast of familiar spaces being invaded or ruptured by the unusual and alien. For all the Doctor is alien, Earth is effectively a home away from home which he constantly returns to.

Vivian Sobchack observed that contemporary American science fiction and horror movies also rely on making the familiar unusual[120]. The motif of Earth as home being ruptured by the alien is a common one in **Doctor Who**, especially during the late 1960s and 1970s. Indeed, one of the most effective **Doctor Who** scenes is the sight of dummies coming to life and bursting from their shop windows to terrorise the passers-by during *Spearhead from Space* (1970). As Jon Arnold observes, 'They are the most logical choice from a gallery of **Doctor Who**'s gallery of monsters' to bring back in *Rose* (2005)

---

[120] Sobchack, Vivian, 'Child/Alien/Father: Patriarchal Crisis and Generic Exchange' in Penley, Constance, Elizabeth Lyon, Lynn Spigel and Janet Bergstrom, eds, *Close Encounters: Film, Feminism and Science Fiction.* p16.

because they are 'a place of domesticity suddenly rendered shockingly alien'[121].

While **Doctor Who** has ranged to the USA in more recent years as the show finally cracked the American market, London remains its focus. The sprawling, multicultural metropolis remains a place with a great significance in the series. It's more than just a domicile for friends and colleagues of the Doctor. Its maze of alleys above ground, and its underground network of tunnels are perfect for invasions, and in *Face the Raven* a sanctuary in which to set a trap. Given Ashildr had set herself the mission to watch for the Doctor, there is no surprise that she based herself there from 1815, the Battle of Waterloo.

Trap Streets and Cartography

CLARA

A trap street. You know, when someone making a map, um a cartographer, uses a fake street, throws it into the mix, names it after one of his kids, or whatever. Then, if the fake street, the trap street, ever shows up on someone else's map, they know their work's been stolen. Clever, right?

DOCTOR

My God. A whole London street just up and disappeared and you lot assumed it's a copyright infringement.

Face the Raven began its creative process under the working title 'Trap Street'. Sarah Dollard says that she cannot remember where she had first heard of trap streets, but thinks she was reminded

---

[121] Arnold, Jon, *The Black Archive #1: Rose*, p30.

about them by a post or comment on Tumblr. She researched them and they stuck with her as a good jumping-off point for a **Doctor Who** story. Steven Moffat agreed when he read Dollard's first pitch, and has enthused about how the idea and subsequent meetings showed him that Dollard gets the romance, humour, cheekiness and horror of the series[122].

A trap street is, as Clara explains to the Doctor, a faked street or feature in a commercially available map to be used to prove copyright infringement should another company steal the original map. Other terms include copyright traps, paper streets, and cartographer's follies. They are usually small and relatively unimportant features, like a ski jump in a small London park, so that the users do not become lost when following the map[123].

Trap streets appear to have emerged from a common practice dating from the 19th century in other reference works, including adding in faked items to encyclopaedias, dictionaries, and scientific journals[124]. Cartography seems to have adopted the secretive practice, but there have been very few successful legal challenges resulting from it. Only one British example has received any form of publicity: the Ordnance Survey (OS) versus the Automobile Association (AA)[125]. For all that

---

[122] Moffat, Steven, **Writing Who** episode 10.

[123] Pedley, Paul, *Essential Law for Information Professionals*, p41.

[124] Maxwell, Rebecca, 'Map Traps: Intentional Mapping Errors to Combat Plagiarism'.

[125] In 2001, the AA paid £20 million in a settlement to the OS after it proved the AA had used detail from OS maps without permission in its travel guides, covering 64 British towns and cities (Jacobs, Frank, 'Help Find London's Missing Map Traps!').

trap streets and the like are meant to be ubiquitous in maps and street directories[126], it has proved to be very difficult to find definitive examples. There are obvious reasons for the secrecy; if they were easy to find the copyright infringer would be able to take steps to minimise risk of their discovery.

As Steven Moffat says, the idea of the fake streets deliberately put in an otherwise accurate map actually being real but hidden from sight is quintessential **Doctor Who**. Our surroundings are our everyday, but what if they hide something magical, or horrific, or just out of the ordinary? That is the very definition of the familiar but odd essence of **Doctor Who**.

The entrance to the trap street in *Face the Raven* was filmed in Westgate Street, Cardiff, and the interior of the alley and dwellings at the Roath Lock Studios. However, the story is set in London and Sarah Dollard did have a part of the city in mind. She imagined it as:

> 'somewhere around Soho or Bloomsbury, basically an old part of London where many of the streets aren't parallel, and there's lot of little nooks and crannies and narrow passageways between buildings, with lots of very different styles of architecture butting up against each other. You can turn a corner on a route you know by heart and find yourself looking up at a building you're certain you've never seen before. There's something magical about that'[127]

---

[126] One claim in the 2005 BBC2 television series, **Map Man**, suggested there were 100 trap streets in the *London A to Z*.
[127] Dollard, Sarah, email interview with the author, 10 November 2017.

During her commentary to *Face the Raven* at the 2016 Gallifrey One convention, Dollard told the audience she imagined the trap street thoroughly. Her vision of it was that the base was Tudor, repaired and added to by lots of people over the ages so that it became a mishmash of new and old, human and alien.

Trap streets, for all that they are well-suited for domestic horror, have only appeared in a few other works of fiction. These include China Miéville's 2010 novel *Kraken*. In it, the trap streets hidden in the *London A to Z* are used by the magical to hide from normal people. Beyond the usual definition of a trap street, a character in the novel muses:

> 'So. Was it that these particular occult streets had been made, then hidden? Their names leaked as traps in an elaborate double-bluff, so that no one could go except those who knew that such traps were actually destinations? Or were there really no streets there when the traps were set? Perhaps these cul-de-sacs were residues, yawned into illicit existence when the atlases were drawn up by liars.'[128]

More recently, in 2013 a Chinese film called *Trap Street* saw map makers attempting to put hidden real streets back on the map and then being trapped; the opposite of the usual definition. The switch allows the film to explore the nature of privacy and surveillance on Chinese society.

Hidden London

> 'Forget the way you usually look at the world. This street's

---

[128] Miéville, China, *Kraken: An Anatomy*, p307.

going to be hiding in plain sight. If you see something unusual or notable, dismiss it. Just keep walking. But if there's a bit of London so unremarkable that you don't even think about it, stop. You could very well be standing right outside a trap street. Count everything that you see, because when you hit the area around a trap street, it's very likely you'll lose count. You'll lose count because the misdirection circuit is creating confusion in your mind. Details won't add up. Reality will have glitches in it.'

[The Doctor]

In contrast to the relatively rare use of trap streets and their ilk in fiction that uses the horror trope of the familiar-yet-different, the concept of an unsettling London hidden within London is far more common. Ross Ruediger observes that:

'In a recent interview with *Raven* scribe Sarah Dollard, she's asked whether the concept was influenced by **Harry Potter**'s Diagon Alley. Being only a peripheral **Potter** fan, this hadn't occurred to me, however the whole idea of a hidden society within the foundations of London is highly reminiscent of Neil Gaiman's **Neverwhere** (which also starred Peter Capaldi), and the notion of sympathetic aliens and monsters hiding from the rest of the world feels equally influenced by Clive Barker's *Nightbreed*, or rather his book, *Cabal*.'[129]

---

[129] Ruediger, Ross, '**Doctor Who** Recap: Tattoo You'. Gaiman novelised his BBC series **Neverwhere** (1996) in the year of broadcast and under the same title. It was also adapted as a radio play in 2013. Barker's film *Nightbreed* (1990) was based on his novella *Cabal*

JK Rowling's **Harry Potter** books, and the films based on them, feature the magical world hidden in plain sight with the 'Muggle' world[130]. Kaitlin Thomas points out a parallel with '**Harry Potter**'s Diagon Alley or even 12 Grimmauld Place, which couldn't be seen unless you already knew its location.'[131] These stories have been phenomenally popular, with a significant crossover audience with **Doctor Who** and members of the production teams, so the similarities are not so surprising. Plus, for all the popularity of that series, the motif of magical hidden places is a common one.

Perhaps unsurprisingly, this motif has appealed to other **Doctor Who** writers. Ben Aaronovitch and Paul Cornell have also written book series that explore the supernatural hiding in modern London. Aaronovitch's **Rivers of London** books, starting with *Rivers of London* (Gollancz, 2011), is now also a comics series written with his fellow **Doctor Who** writer Andrew Cartmel. The stories feature a magical hidden London and are narrated by PC Peter Grant. Cornell's series follows a small Metropolitan Police team dubbed **The Shadow Police** as they try to bring law and order to London's hidden monsters and creatures. In development since at least 2008, the first book, *London Falling*, was published by Tor in 2012. In a rather bold move, the second of the series, *The Severed Streets*, features Neil Gaiman as a major character. Gaiman, of course, wrote *Neverwhere* (1996), which as Ruediger mentions takes the reader through the cracks into an underground world full of monks, knights, monsters, and others.

(1988).
[130] Beginning with *Harry Potter and the Philosopher's Stone* (1997), filmed under the same title in 2001.
[131] Thomas, 'Swan Song'.

London has long been a gateway to other worlds in popular fiction. JM Barrie's play (1904) and novel (1911) about *Peter Pan and Wendy* launches from Kensington Gardens and Bloomsbury to Neverland. CS Lewis wrote a prequel to his *The Lion, The Witch and the Wardrobe* (1950), *The Magician's Nephew* (1955) in which young neighbours Polly and Digory are tricked by Digory's Uncle Andrew into leaving their London homes to journey by magic to Narnia. On Digory's return, he plants a magical apple tree, which when it topples he makes into the wardrobe the Pevensie children later find and use as the entrance to Narnia.

All of these stories take the familiar and either twist or add the unfamiliar to it. That is, of course, one of the ways in which **Doctor Who** has captured and kept its audience over the decades. As John Tulloch and Manuel Alvarado note, 'Unlike a lot of popular science fiction, the diegetic world of [**Doctor Who**'s] characters was not simply "displaced" in some other time or place. It was located, insistently, in the present.'[132]

In *The Closed Space*, Manuel Aguirre explored the ideas of space in the realms of the family, the home, and other familiar territory, and how they are used in the storytelling that characterises horror[133]. Vivian Sobchack, too, noted that US science fiction/horror movies like *Close Encounters of the Third Kind* (1977), *ET: The Extra-Terrestrial* (1982), *Starman* (1984) and *The Terminator* (1984) tend to be set in a contemporary time and amongst familiar surroundings to

---

[132] Tulloch and Alvarado, *The Unfolding Text*, p16.
[133] Aguirre, Manuel, *The Closed Space: Horror Literature and Western Symbolism.*

increase the feeling of dislocation and invasion that occurs when the aliens or monsters arrive[134]. **Doctor Who** is not pure science fiction or space opera and over the decades, writers and directors have borrowed symbolism and motifs from genres and subgenres including horror, and usually used the terror of enclosed space: the Edwardian lighthouse featured in *Horror of Fang Rock* (1977) is one classic example.

Warrick notes that in science fiction and other tales of the weird, supernatural, or magical, there needs to be some kind of mechanism for the necessary dislocation that enables the reader or television/film audience member to more readily suspend their disbelief and enter the fiction[135]. In *Face the Raven* the misdirection circuit and the use of the retcon drug are both mechanisms used to convince the audience that it is possible that a hidden refugee camp full of aliens and monsters could exist in contemporary London.

Face the Raven is not the first time we see aliens hiding themselves in London in **Doctor Who**. The Great Intelligence made the robot Yeti use the Underground to move around in *The Web of Fear* (1968); the Cybermen used London's sewer system in *The Invasion* (1968) and *Attack of the Cybermen* (1985). Others like the Slitheen in *Aliens of London / World War Three* (2005) disguise themselves as humans who infiltrate Parliament and Number 10 Downing Street. The Zygons did similarly in their return stories in 2013 and 2015, having been seen in Scotland in *Terror of the Zygons* (1975). The tension in these stories builds from not knowing who is a Zygon and who is human – in *The Zygon Invasion / The Zygon Inversion* until the last

---

[134] Sobchack, Vivian, 'Child/Alien/Father', p16.
[135] Warrick, *The Cybernetic Imagination in Science Fiction*, pp82–83.

moment, and with the Osgoods, never. In *Face the Raven*, Ashildr the Mayor refers to the fragile peace that exists between the Zygons and humans on Earth when she explains to the Doctor and Clara how she runs the street.

London's history and geography both lend themselves to these tales. There has been a human settlement on the banks of the Thames river since prehistoric times, and waves of invasion or revolution have shaped it. It's been destroyed, or near enough, several times, and rebuilt. It is not a planned city, though parts were. It's a conglomerate of different villages and estates, all quite different from each other. It has also expanded as the population has.

A Refuge from the Doctor

'I guarantee the safety of Clara Oswald. She will be under my personal protection. That is absolute.'

[Ashildr]

Obviously, the Doctor has made numerous enemies over the years, and he and his friends have thwarted hundreds of alien invasions. With UNIT and Torchwood on the lookout for more, Ashildr has her work cut out for her in running her refuge, especially since she set it up in 1815 or thereabouts. During the 1800s Ashildr disappeared from the Doctor's watchful eye, until she resurfaces in a picture that Clara shows the Doctor on her phone when he returns to contemporary London at the end of *The Woman Who Lived*. The photograph shows Ashildr in the background, but looking directly at the camera. Ashildr confirms to the Doctor during *Face the Raven* that she had deliberately been photographed in order to attract his attention.

Most of the aliens and other non-human creatures Ashildr has allowed refuge appear as human to the Doctor and Clara, and through them the audience. The exceptions are the Janus. Rigsy, though, can see the reality through glitches in the perception field generated by the lurk worms, which allows the audience to see glimpses. Through that, and the Doctor's ability to see through the filter, we see a Sontaran, an Ood caring for a Cyberman, and that the Mayoral police are Judoon. There are a few difficult to identify, and both Rump and Kabel are creatures we have not seen before. The Doctor says that he has counted 27 separate species on the street, of which 15 were aggressive. Sarah Dollard told the audience at the Gallifrey One live commentary for *Face the Raven* that an early draft of her script included Adipose-driven little bicycles, but these were the first to be cut. As Simon Brew points out, 'No wonder it's described as "the most dangerous street in London"[136].' However, Emily Asher-Perrin argues that:

> 'Mayor Me is trying to do something good with her influence and endless experience, but she is essentially wielding martial law over these beings, with no recourse for unacceptable behaviour aside from death[137].'

Justice on the street is brutal and meted out quickly by Ashildr using the Quantum Shade. We witness an inhabitant having his chronolock count down to zero and rather than face the Raven, he runs. The Raven hunts him down and kills him in front of the residents of the street and the Doctor, Clara and Rigsy – for the crime of stealing medicine for his life partner. It is a scene that demonstrates clearly

---

[136] Brew, '*Face the Raven* Review'.
[137] Asher-Perrin, 'Let Me Be Brave'.

just how dangerous the Quantum Shade is, and how hopeless Rigsy's situation seems. No one can escape the Quantum Shade once the chronolock reaches zero.

Steven Moffat suggested the trap street should house a refugee camp for aliens[138]. The idea for the story of a murder plot that the Doctor and Clara need to investigate developed through meetings between Moffat, Dollard, the script editors and others. **Doctor Who** under Moffat didn't operate a US-style writers' room approach, but it has always been collaborative, with many people coming up with ideas that are incorporated at various stages in the production of a story. Things can change even when filming; for example, Clara's scream as the Quantum Shade reaches her was recorded but in post-production the team decided to make the scream silent. They felt that Jenna Coleman's scream was devastating, but the silent scream would still punch the emotions.

Some of the aliens living in the trap street are not antagonists on the run to escape justice, but instead are victims seeking refuge against injustice. This includes Anah and Anahson, a pair of Janus who have escaped their captors and the abuse they suffered as slaves, forced to see into the future for their masters. It is no surprise that Ashildr uses Rigsy's alleged murder of the innocent Anah as bait and hook for the Doctor.

Gender politics figure heavily in this plot strand. Female Janus can see into the future, but males cannot. Anah disguised her daughter as a boy, Anahson, to protect her from those who seek those who can see the future. Unfortunately, a whole scene between Clara and

---

[138] Dollard, Sarah, **Writing Who** episode 10.

Anah about the differences in how women are treated from men, and the reasons behind why important decisions are taken, was cut the day before it was due to be shot[139]. What remains is a smaller scene, but it still makes the point that boys are often safer in dangerous situations. The Janus also raise the issue of time and question how history can be interpreted, picking up on themes discussed in the previous chapter. They have two faces, one facing forward that can see the future and one at the back that can see into the past. Anahson struggles to 'read' the Doctor, which means that she cannot in fact help untangle the plot in time for the Doctor to thwart Ashildr's plans in trapping him.

Given the range of aliens living in the street, most of which are battle-hardened warriors trapped in a less than ideal situation or traumatised refugees far from home, the peace the Mayor has brought is fragile. If there is one characteristic of monsters in **Doctor Who**, their universal objective is to either subjugate or, more likely, totally destroy their enemies. As a result, these monsters have many enemies and exhibit great ruthlessness and often cunning. When we do see them team up in a grand alliance, it's to eliminate the danger the Doctor poses them by trapping him in the Pandorica[140]. Their involvement in alliances and peace agreements is fraught with paranoia and danger. They tend to see the universe as a zero-sum game, and because they are out to get everyone else they assume everyone else is out to get them. Add into the mix a sense of vulnerability through being hunted on Earth and often some kind of injury, and the situation is extremely volatile. Ashildr enforces a type

---

[139] Dollard, Gallifrey One live commentary.
[140] *The Pandorica Opens* (2010).

73

of honour amongst them, but it is mostly driven by fear. That's fear of death, discovery, and above all fear of losing their place of safety. Ashildr knows she has to be brutal to keep the peace. Rump says that justice needs to be seen to be done to Rigsy, and quickly, because otherwise the barely suppressed paranoia and violence will erupt as suspicion will inevitably turn inward to the residents.

Simply having the Doctor in their midst, with the alleged murderer Rigsy, threatens that fragile stability. As noted in the previous chapter, the fact that Ashildr effectively uses a young black man to stir up a volatile population picks up events in the real world that on varying levels for the audience will illustrate just how ruthless Ashildr is[141]. The casting of two black actors as the escaped Janus slaves, Anah and Anahson, reinforces the connections with real world racism and Ashildr's cynical use of them in her plot to ensnare both the Doctor and Clara. However, as with Rigsy, there is no overt reference. Catherine Gee writes that:

> 'Its poignant allegories of the perils of a society run by fear and the barbarity of capital punishment were more subtle than the ISIL comparisons of *The Zygon Invasion* / [*The Zygon*] *Inversion*[142].'

This is not the only real-world theme in *Face the Raven*; others are explored in the next section.

A Refuge from the World

> 'There have always been rumours. Stories passed from

---

[141] Asher-Perrin, 'Let Me Be Brave'.
[142] Gee, Catherine, '**Doctor Who**: *Face the Raven* – Clara Dies, So Will Maisie Williams Be The New Companion?'

traveller to traveller, mutterings about hidden streets, secret pockets of alien life right here on Earth. Like a smuggler's cove, only not a cove, because it's right here. Right in the middle of the capital.'

[The Doctor]

Face the Raven was made and first aired in the midst of a world-wide refugee crisis and extensively publicised political discourse against migration generally. Emily Asher-Perrin wrote that 'the fact that Me is running a refugee camp is extremely topical right now [...] And to **Doctor Who**'s credit, these aliens are not demonized for their plight, distrusting as they are. We see how hard they must work to survive, how carefully their lives are policed.'[143]

Henri Lefebvre's work concentrated on exploring the notion of 'social space', returning to and engaging with philosophical questions connected to space. He criticised preceding accounts as 'mere descriptions which never achieve analytical, much less theoretical, status'[144]. Lefebvre began his *The Production of Space* with the observation that 'Not so many years ago, the word "space" had a strictly geometrical meaning: the idea it evoked was simply that of an empty area'[145]. He reminds us that there is much more than one space: there is physical space (both nature and the cosmos); mental space (logical and formal abstractions) and social space[146]. Social space includes 'the space of social practice, the space occupied by

---

[143] Asher-Perrin, 'Let Me Be Brave'.
[144] Lefebvre, Henri, *The Production of Space*, p7.
[145] Lefebvre, Henri, *The Production of Space*, p1.
[146] Lefebvre, Henri, *The Production of Space*, p11.

sensory phenomena, including products of the imagination such as projects and projections, symbols and utopias'[147]. **Doctor Who** engages on some level with each of these spaces: stories are often set in physical spaces; some are set in mental space; and *Face the Raven* is set in social space. It's a particular type of social space, too: the social space of desperate and fearful refugees.

During the 2010s, elements of British politics and the media turned up the volume again on anti-refugee rhetoric, this time against Muslims fleeing Arab and Middle Eastern conflict. Not for the first time, the fear of refugees hiding terrorists was raised. When *The Zygon Invasion / The Zygon Inversion* was first broadcast on 31 October and 7 November 2015, it was after a summer with a worsening refugee crisis at Calais and in and around the Mediterranean. At the same time, the terrorist group Daesh[148] was prominent in headlines and in mid-November 2015 claimed responsibility for a series of co-ordinated terrorist attacks in Paris. Right-wing politicians in several countries, including the UK, issued numerous claims that Daesh terrorists were hiding amongst the refugees. These **Doctor Who** Zygon stories explored the strains on refugee aliens living in a forced peace and what happens when a group radicalises among those refugees. The stories, while not subtle, do handle the complexities with a degree of sensitivity. They also deal with the effect of forgetting recent history, in this case enforced to protect UNIT's Black Archive and the fragile peace between humans and Zygons on Earth. Ashildr compares her refugee

---

[147] Lefebvre, Henri, *The Production of Space*, p12.
[148] Also known as the Islamic State in the Levant (ISIL) or the Islamic State in Syria (ISIS). 'Daesh', a phonetic transcription of the Arabic acronym, is the term preferred by the UK Government.

solution to that of the fragile peace brokered by the Doctor and UNIT. Kaitlin Thomas argues that:

> 'I think it's incredibly important [for] **Doctor Who**, a series that routinely features different races and one that has promoted peace and promoted peaceful resolutions to war and conflict to tackle this topic. We saw it with the Zygons and we saw it here, too, and the fact that it's even being discussed is a big deal. The only real problem is that it also occurred in the same episode as Clara's death, and so it was a little overshadowed.'[149]

There are two things about London that make it exactly the right place for a secret refugee camp for aliens. Firstly, London is the type of place where it is easy to imagine such places being able to exist. In the City of London itself, the Square Mile, there are nooks and crannies galore, and when you do turn a corner past some modern concrete and glass you are in an alley surrounded by buildings that are much, much older. For all the development going on, there are still passageways and narrow walkways in Soho and Bloomsbury and all around the West End and quite a bit of the East End. Then there is the Underground, and disused tunnels all around the capital. As already explored, it is no wonder London has long been used as a setting for supernatural and magical stories, most often hidden from the ordinary populations.

Secondly, London is a migrant city and has been for millennia. Its population is richly diverse and mostly cosmopolitan. It is easy to imagine that that diversity would make it easy to hide in such a city.

---

[149] Thomas, 'Swan Song'.

Voluntary migration as we know of it now was rare for much of the city's history. Most often people were forced to flee their homes because of war or persecution, or were brought to the city as the British empire expanded. Relatively large numbers from South Asia (mostly from modern India), China and the African continent arrived and settled in London. One major wave of refugees that made their mark on London in the 17th century was the Huguenots from France[150]. Approximately 40 to 50,000 French Protestants arrived, a large number during that time, taking up the sanctuary offered to them by King Charles II in about 1670, many of them in the East End of London.

There have been multiple waves of large groups of refugees who settled in London over the centuries, including approximately 120,000 of the two million Jews escaping Tsarist Russia between 1881 and 1914, thousands of people after the Second World War from the new Commonwealth to work in manual jobs, and numerous refugees from various wars. According to Home Office records, applications for asylum in the UK rose in the late 1990s, peaking at the turn of the millennium, and then dropped in 2004-05[151]. Many were from Afghanistan and Iraq, and more recently Syria.

Refugees and asylum seekers are not the only people to migrate to the UK in general, or London in particular. People who choose to migrate do so for many reasons. The UK is not the only European

---

[150] Cooray Smith, James, *The Black Archive #2: The Massacre*, explores the **Doctor Who** story that involves the events that spark the Huguenot migration.
[151] Asylum applications and initial decisions for main applicants, by country of nationality. Home Office. 27 August 2015.

country that was a colonial power up to and including the 20th century, but it did have the largest empire. There are people from the former colonies who seek to live in the 'mother country' for the experience, for better jobs and economic prospects, and/or for a better life in general. Some move permanently, others move temporarily.

Australians are one such group of many, and Sarah Dollard is among their number. In her response to a reader of her Tumblr blog asking for advice on how to become a writer for **Doctor Who**, Dollard commented that it is useful to live and work in the UK[152]. Dollard had, of course, established a television writing career in Australia before moving to the UK where she had almost to start afresh, working as part of a team on **Merlin** (2008-12) and **Primeval** (2007-11) before landing a commission for **Being Human** (2008-13) and then **Doctor Who**. Dollard discusses immigration-related issues on social media, and while *Face the Raven* features refugees it does not really examine the refugee or migrant experience.

Not everyone in London welcomes refugees or migrants. At the turn of the 20th century, immigration was reduced by the Aliens Act, 1905 and virtually curtailed by the Aliens Restriction Act, 1914. Following World War Two and the subsequent influx of people from around the world, several different acts came into power to control numbers of migrants. In the late 1960s and early 1970s the political backlash against migrants, particularly those who were black and of other ethnic minorities, escalated, and then receded in the years following the Race Discrimination Act coming into force in 1965. These waves

---

[152] Dollard, Sarah, '"My dream is to be a screenwriter (especially for **Doctor Who**). Do you have any advice?" Yes it turns out I do.'

of anti-immigrant feeling continue to peak and trough, and not always in sync with actual refugee or migrant numbers. Fear of violence emanating from larger groups of refugees or migrants – sometimes based on fact, other times not – has driven reactions from Londoners, through both violent action and legislation. The anti-French sentiment in the 17th century is captured on the plaque to the Monument raised in memory to the Great Fire of 1666; popular opinion had it that the fire had been caused by French migrants. For much of the 20th century Irish migrants faced various forms of discrimination, not always directly as a result of the violent campaigns waged in England for Irish self-rule.

Face the Raven's refugee camp in a trap street hides real monsters as well as victims, but this story is not the story of violence and terror against their hosts. It is rather the tale of a trap set and sprung, and through Ashildr and Clara trying to second guess the Doctor, a tale that results in the tragedy of Clara's death and anguish for Ashildr. For, while Ashildr's trap was successful in snaring the Doctor for the Time Lords, she had been careful to rig it so that neither Anah or Rigsy would have died. Clara's death was therefore unnecessary and, by virtue of that, a true tragedy.

CHAPTER 4: DEATH AND THE RAVEN

'She died for who she was, and who she loved. She fell where she stood. It was sad, and it was beautiful, and it is over. We have no right to change who she was.'

[Ashildr, *Hell Bent*]

For all that *Face the Raven* explores a community of refugee aliens hidden in London, the story is about a trap set by Ashildr to catch the Doctor and send him back to the Time Lords. The trap is the apparent (but non-existent) murder of one of the innocent victims living in the refugee camp and the capital sentence imposed on Rigsy. It's successful in so far as the Doctor is caught and transported away from Earth, but Ashildr's plans to leave no one physically harmed are shattered when Clara interferes and is executed in the place of Rigsy.

Clara's sacrifice for someone who wasn't actually in real mortal peril is the central tragedy of the story – a tragedy in that she attempts to emulate the Doctor, believes she has succeeded, and then is shown to have failed with no 'fix' available. She is a good liar who means well, and she is brave, but she is ultimately the most ordinary of young women catapulted into the most impossible of situations.

As for Ashildr, she is motivated to rid her world of the Doctor, who she sees as responsible for causing Earth a lot of grief, for all his attempts to protect the planet. She takes the chance given to her by the Time Lords, as we later learn in *Heaven Sent*, which gives her the means to trap the Doctor in her street. She has the Quantum Shade and chronolock, weapons she uses to keep the peace in her dangerous little community, and which serve as a particularly useful tool to construct her trap for the Doctor. Death does not come instantly to those sentenced, which means there is a period of time for the Doctor to intervene, and for Ashildr to reveal that, as no one has been murdered, Rigsy's death sentence cannot be carried out.

Ashildr's destiny is made once the 12th Doctor sees fit to grant her immortality. The two attempt across time to manage each other – and in the midst of this, Clara is killed by the Quantum Shade when she takes on Rigsy's death sentence in a way that cannot be altered.

This chapter returns to the ideas about death contained in *Face the Raven* and **Doctor Who** more broadly. Not just any death, but specifically murder and retribution, and some of the symbolism associated with ravens and death.

The Quantum Shade as Raven

'A raven is both ubiquitous and creepy – perfect for a **Doctor Who** monster!'[153]

[Sarah Dollard]

Sarah Dollard told the audience at the Gallifrey One live commentary on her first **Doctor Who** story that her early drafts of the script described the Quantum Shade as a gun that painted a target on someone's back, creating a bait for a monster. She says, 'The tattoo came to me as a thing someone can control.'[154] In contrast, anyone can just pick up and use a gun. The idea of the gun with a delayed death is reminiscent of the IMIPAK (Induced Molecular Instability Projector and Key) weapon in the **Blake's 7** episode *Weapon* (1979), but there is no suggestion Dollard's initial Quantum Shade idea was

---

[153] Dollard, email interview with the author.
[154] Dollard, Gallifrey One live commentary.

based on this.

The Quantum Shade appears in the televised *Face the Raven* as a swirly black tattoo, almost Nordic in design, around Ashildr the Mayor's neck. When activated, it curls up and leaves her skin in a black smoke form, apparently to join a caged raven that can escape to find its quarry. In this it conjures the meaning of 'quantum' – as in the branch of theoretical physics that allows for particles to be in two states at the same time – and 'shade' in the sense of a shadow or ghost. We never see Ashildr communicate directly with it, but the way she talks about it throughout the story suggests a clearly defined legal arrangement based on a contract made each time she as the Mayor passes sentence of death. If Rump had not told Clara about how the chronolock tattoo can be passed to another willing to take it, or had Clara not acted upon that information, then it is highly likely that Ashildr would have commuted Rigsy's sentence once the Doctor had the teleport bracelet on.

The Quantum Shade is linked to another strange type of tattoo: the chronolock. Again, it is the familiar yet odd that attracts the Doctor and Clara into the adventure when Rigsy calls to tell them about a tattoo. At first the Doctor dismisses the ordinary-sounding story as boring; but when he realises what it truly is, he immediately and vocally changes his mind. This should have been a clue that the Doctor knew far more about it than he let on, but instead the adventure of hunting down the trap street takes over and the gravity of the danger glossed over until it is too late for Clara. That moment of the Doctor's knowing gravitas is lost in the usual exhilaration of rushing about to save people's lives. If Clara had spotted it, understood it, interrogated it then perhaps her later error could have been averted. However, that is another thing about the Doctor that forever makes him different to his companions: the vast knowledge gained from millennia of travels and adventures.

Dollard went on to tell the Gallifrey One audience that she considered what would be scary in a **Doctor Who** way but hadn't been done before, and thought about something rushing right at a person that they cannot escape. She thought of a bird: a big, black bird with a beak that means business. Dan Martin, critic for *The Guardian*, writes, 'death-by-raven is surely one of the most unsettling we have seen for some time, exacerbated by the muting out of Clara's death screams.'[155]

In answer to a specific question for this book, Dollard says:

> 'a quantum shade is an alien shape-shifting creature so it doesn't always look like a raven, that's just the form it takes on earth. Originally the raven was a crow, but that changed almost by accident at some point during the drafting process, I think because a raven is easier to train and have on a set. Both birds symbolise bad luck and death, and come with unsettling baggage from so many stories that associate them with horror and graveyards, etc., so they seemed an ideal form for the quantum shade. A raven is both ubiquitous and creepy – perfect for a **Doctor Who** monster!'

The Quantum Shade as raven is, as Dollard alludes to, the very definition of that similar but different motif that permeates all through **Doctor Who**.

---

[155] Martin, '*Face the Raven*'.

Ravens

'And the Raven, never flitting, still is sitting, still is sitting
On the pallid bust of Pallas just above my chamber door;
And his eyes have all the seeming of a demon's that is
    dreaming,
And the lamp-light o'er him streaming throws his shadow on
    the floor;
And my soul from out that shadow that lies floating on the
    floor
Shall be lifted – nevermore!'
[Edgar Allan Poe, 'The Raven']

A raven is the perfect bird for the Quantum Shade. Big enough to be scary as it rushes towards the condemned, but small enough and smart enough to be amenable to handling. Ravens, and other members of the corvid family, are associated in contemporary popular culture with death through poems such as Edgar Allan Poe's and the fact that they are carrion eaters. Furthermore, they are associated with battlefields and warfare in Irish mythology that carries through to Arthurian legend, where they feature as the army of Sir Owain as told in the medieval prose tale 'The Dream of Rhonabwy'. The birds were also a feature in the aftermath of the great battles in Europe throughout its history. Now, they often appear in the background in horror movies, cawing menacingly. However, the birds have a far richer cultural history than simply as a horror motif.

Dan Martin was one reviewer of the story who noted the association of ravens with Ashildr's Viking origins:

It surely cannot be a coincidence that Ashildr's old godhead

Odin was in mythology accompanied by two ravens, Hugin and Mugin, even though Me can barely remember her old life as Ashildr. Maybe she read about them in her journals?[156]

Indeed, the two ravens served Odin as either his eyes and ears, or as his thought and memory – an echo with Ashildr's own memory loss. Ravens are also often depicted as messengers, and Hugin and Mugin are depicted as bringing Odin news from Midgard[157]. Ravens were common for Vikings in general, as carried through to being a symbol on the coat of arms for the Isle of Man, which was a former Viking colony. One Viking, the perhaps mythological Ragnar Loðbrok, had a banner with a raven motif that would flutter to indicate he would be victorious in battle, but hang limp if he were to lose. The Old Norse word for raven was *hrafn,* and was frequently used in conjunction with other words for bloodshed and battle[158]. We can speculate that the Quantum Shade adopted the shape of a raven for Ashildr in relation to a residual memory.

Ravens have appeared in numerous myths and legends the world over, so it is not surprising that they are used in more recent fantasy series like **Game of Thrones**. While ravens are generally used as messengers in the world of Westeros, the three-eyed raven seen by Bran Stark in visions brings a more esoteric communication. The name 'Bran' translates from medieval Irish as raven, and is also the name of one of the Welsh gods. In the *Mabinogion*, a collection of medieval Welsh texts that includes 'The Dream of Rhonabwy'

---

[156] Martin, '*Face the Raven*'.
[157] Avia, 'Raven Symbolism and Symbolic Meaning of Ravens.'
[158] Britt, Hugo Edward, *The Beasts of Battle: Associative Connections of the Wolf, Raven And Eagle in Old English Poetry*, p121.

mentioned earlier, the god Bran's head was buried in the White Hill of London to protect the city against invasion. As for the ordinary ravens' role in Westeros, this could be George RR Martin being inspired by ancient Greek legends where ravens were Apollo's messengers on Earth – though they also appear as messengers to survivors of dead heroes in Serbian epic poems including 'Tsar Lazar and Tsarina Militsa' and 'The Battle of Mishar'[159]. In other cultures and stories ravens denote great wisdom[160], which is what the Three-Eyed Raven ultimately imparts to Bran in **Game of Thrones**.

There is a legend that states that the Kingdom of England will fall if the ravens resident at the Tower of London leave. Stories abound that at least six ravens have resided in the castle grounds for centuries, but there is no proof of that. The story goes that the first reference to the prophecy dates to Charles II who refused to destroy the ravens because of the legend, but there is no contemporary record of it. There is pictorial and literary proof of ravens living in the Tower grounds dating from a list of the ravens' names held by the Tower from 1880, and then an 1883 newspaper, and then increasing references through to the 20th century. It is likely that some of the Yeoman Warders had dramatised the likely existence of ravens around public execution sites to tourists who had started to visit the attraction. Ravens were very likely to have been a common sight around the meat markets of London, including the Eastcheap area

---

[159] Matthias, John, and Vladeta Vuckovic, trans, 'The Battle of Kosovo: Serbian Epic Poems'.
[160] Avia, 'Raven Symbolism and Symbolic Meaning of Ravens.'

near to the Tower[161].

Aside from *Face the Raven*, ravens have appeared a few times before in **Doctor Who**'s history. With UNIT and the Black Archive having moved into the Tower of London it was inevitable for the resident birds to make an appearance. Kate Stewart did not disappoint, and claimed they ran on batteries during *The Day of the Doctor*. Previously in *The Power of Three* (2012) they were jokingly called 'ravens of death'.

Ravens also appeared during season 16 (the 'Key to Time' season), and later in the Black Guardian trilogy[162]. In an apparent nod to the story of the Great Flood, the Black Guardian wore a raven on his head and the White Guardian wore a dove. According to *Genesis* 8:7-12, Noah first released a raven to see if the land was again habitable, but the bird didn't leave the ark, which led to it being distrusted. Noah then despatched a dove, which returned with an olive branch; hence doves remain a symbol of peace.

Ravens feature in *The Stones of Blood* (1978) where Leonard de Vries of the British Institute of Druidic Studies keeps one in his home because of their association with the Celtic goddess Cailleach. Harking back to Odin's use of two ravens as his eyes and ears, de Vries and his fellow druids believe the raven to be the eyes of the Cailleach. Ravens are used to great effect in the story, with a number perching on the TARDIS when it lands.

---

[161] Jerome, Fiona, *Tales from the Tower*, pp148-9, and Sax, Boria, 'The Tower Ravens: Invented Tradition, Fakelore, or Modern Myth', *Storytelling, Self, and Society* vol 6 #3, p234.
[162] *Mawdryn Undead, Terminus* and *Enlightenment* (all 1983).

Ravens live in most of the northern hemisphere, across Europe from the Arctic to the Mediterranean, and across the Americas. Varieties also live in Australia and New Zealand. There is little to distinguish them from crows except their general size, ravens being larger. They are omnivores that include carrion in their diet, but they are also skilled hunters. They have been observed working in teams to bring down prey much larger than a bird their size could on its own[163].

Recent studies have suggested that ravens are particularly intelligent and able to distinguish and remember others (humans or ravens) who give them some kind of advantage[164]. In a series of tests to determine ability to plan for the future and delaying gratification to barter, ravens performed better than human toddlers and great apes doing the same tests[165]. The Raven Master at the Tower of London has demonstrated on Twitter and other social media several behaviours of the ravens under his care that suggest a high level of intelligence. These include crooning and gentle nipping to encourage continued stroking of their beaks, as well as playing dead for attention.

That intelligence has been seen in a variety of film and television productions. Ravens do not take as much training as other birds and tend to repeat their performance for multiple takes without much fuss. This behaviour is unlike owls, which when used as messenger birds in the **Harry Potter** films tended to not be able to repeat takes

---

[163] 'Common Raven', *National Geographic Online*.
[164] Gibbens, Sarah, 'Ravens Hold Grudges Against Cheaters'.
[165] Montanari, Shaena, 'We Knew Ravens Are Smart. But Not This Smart.'

so easily and wasted time. As Sarah Dollard observes, during the production of her script the type of bird changed to a raven because they are easier to wrangle on set[166].

Death and Doctor Who

'Everybody lives, Rose! Just this once, everybody lives.'

[The Doctor, *The Doctor Dances* (2005)]

Here is a startling fact about **Doctor Who**. With the exception of *The Edge of Destruction* (1964), there isn't a single story of the television series from *An Unearthly Child* to *The Empty Child* / *The Doctor Dances* (2005) that doesn't have a death in it[167]. Not only that, during the very first adventure following the TARDIS leaving the junkyard with the abducted teachers, Ian Chesterton and Barbara Wright, the Doctor nearly kills an injured caveman while he, Susan, Ian and Barbara are running for their lives. Not because the caveman is a direct threat to them, but because he is slowing them down. Ian stops the Doctor, but there is no remorse shown by the old man who abducted them. That is not the last time in the show's 55 years that the Doctor is casual about killing and death.

However, audiences remember his posturing about individual

---

[166] Dollard, Gallifrey One live commentary.
[167] Carrol, David, 'Death' in Burk and Smith?, eds, *Time Unincorporated Volume 2*, p331. This may depend to some extent on what counts as 'alive' in the first place.

deaths[168] and preventing genocidal massacres[169], but tend to gloss over when he is responsible for advocating the same[170]. Lou Anders writes:

> 'when you get right down to it, **Doctor Who** is a series about the battle between good and evil. That the front line of this battle takes place in the head of the same man, that's what I find so compelling.'[171]

We see this time and time again throughout the whole series. The seventh Doctor is an obvious example, but so are the treatment of both the Valeyard and the War Doctor as separate characters in conflict with the current Doctor, and the 11th Doctor battling the Cybercontroller during *Nightmare in Silver* (2013) so that we and Clara are never quite sure which is him and which is the Cyberman – all these are but a tiny sample.

Even though countless numbers of people and aliens have died in **Doctor Who**, death's ramifications are rarely dealt with in the television series. Following Adric's death in *Earthshock* audiences saw the Doctor, Nyssa and Tegan react with grief, and the production

---

[168] For repeated examples, Davros is the extreme. Following *Genesis of the Daleks* when the fourth Doctor fails to stop the Daleks from ever existing, there are numerous other chances to kill Davros to save millions, but that chance is never actually taken.
[169] For example, when the third Doctor stops the Brigadier and UNIT from wiping out *The Silurians* (1970).
[170] For example, against the Sea Devils (1972), and also the destruction of Skaro in *Remembrance of the Daleks*.
[171] Anders, Lou, 'The Doctor's Darker Nature', in Burk and Smith?, eds, *Time Unincorporated Volume 2*, p324.

team marked the event with silent end credits rolling over a still of his shattered star of mathematical excellence. However, in the next episode everything had returned to normal, with only the occasional reminder of his existence and death[172]. As Kaitlin Thomas writes: 'Death happens to you, but its effects are felt by the ones you leave behind.'[173]

The show has always had companions leave, and new ones replace those now gone. The Doctor, too, has regenerated enough times for the audience to become used to no one actor retaining the role for any real length of time. Of course, each Doctor attracts new viewers and fans and there is always a group who identify strongly with 'their' Doctor. All this change makes **Doctor Who** not really the type of show to raise and answer questions about death, as in the here-today, gone-tomorrow, permanently dead type of death.

The constant departing and arriving of actors and main characters reflects the intertwining of escape and belonging central to the series. Elspeth Probyn plays with the paradoxical desires of simultaneously seeking home and escape: in her words, 'belonging brings forth images of leaving, carting one's possessions and baggage from place to place [...] while belonging may make one think of arriving, it also carries the scent of departures'[174].

Doctor Who is at its heart an adventure series. It is about discovery as much as it is about the struggle against oppression, or the battle between good and evil. The thrill and excitement of meeting new

---

[172] *Time Flight* (1982), *Terminus*, and *Resurrection of the Daleks* (1984).
[173] Thomas, 'Swan Song'.
[174] Probyn, 'Queer Belongings', p2.

people, seeing new places and things drives the narrative of the series, regardless of the specific situations the main characters find themselves in. The ability of the characters and story to go anywhere and anytime is arguably the main hook that has caught and continues to catch audiences and keep their interest across the five decades it has run to date. That adventure is addictive. Intoxicating. Exciting. Dangerous. Full of change, including that of the titular character and the actors who play the role, and the risks that go with all that change.

For all the romance of adventure and the thrill of defeating evil, travelling with the Doctor is a dangerous business. The monsters confronted mostly want to exterminate, assimilate, or subjugate others. They target individuals, small groups, entire planets, or galaxies, or even the universe. The Doctor has always striven to thwart those ambitions; the character taking on the struggle as though it is the weight of the universe and all of time. As the series ages along with the titular character so does that burden grow. Over the 55 years since its beginning the Doctor has struggled more and more with those burdens, and the toll taken by the character's actions during the Time War in particular has affected the narrative flow across many stories. The reverberation of acts regretted permeates so many stories in big and small ways. Those repercussions emerge also in the way that those affected by the Doctor act, often inspired by their friend. Occasionally they act directly in what they perceive to be the opposite of how the Doctor might act in the same situation, and at other times they just act.

The Doctor's companions, by virtue of sharing those adventures, also share in carrying that burden despite the Doctor's best efforts to shield them from it. There is the pain of impossible choices, and the mounting toll of stress, physical and mental. We should not ignore that those monsters have a tendency to capture the Doctor's friends, and are usually brutal, torturing the companions either physically or psychologically, or both. Sometimes that brutality is to obtain information, but often it is to trap the Doctor, which must lead some of them to suffer guilt. Either way, the harm done to the people who travel with the Doctor is immense, even though it is rarely played out in the stories shown. More often than not the build-up of the near-constant levels of physical and emotional stress isn't seen to take its toll on those in the TARDIS, but when it does it adds to the drama of the series. A stand out example is Tegan's emotional break down in the final episode of *Resurrection of the Daleks* (1984) that precipitates her departure from the TARDIS. Adric's death, and the many deaths that Tegan witnessed before and afterwards, are what drives her to leave the Doctor for once and for all. But leaving the TARDIS means she leaves the adventure, that addictive adrenaline rush.

Death is, of course, a possibility that the Doctor's companions live with. The risk of it happening to them is high, but before Steven Moffat took over as Producer and main writer for the show in 2010 it had only actually happened to three companions.

Death in Steven Moffat's Doctor Who

'In the end, everyone does this alone.'

[Clara]

Before Steven Moffat took over from Russell T Davies as showrunner of **Doctor Who** he wrote the highly acclaimed two-part story *The Empty Child / The Doctor Dances*. In the second of these two episodes, the Doctor exclaims to Rose that no one has died during the course of the story.

As noted previously, Tulloch and Alvarado observed that **Doctor Who**'s 'incoming producers make judgements as to which audience groups they feel the programme is under-serving when they are considering what their own particular "signature" will be'[175]. Moffat not only played with the way time could be used in storytelling, as seen in the second chapter of this monograph, he played with notions of death and resurrection repeatedly. Amy Pond's husband, Rory Williams, dies many times during the series. His deaths are often sacrifices to help others, and then he is brought back from the dead, eventually and finally resurrected to live out the rest of his life with Amy in *The Angels Take Manhattan* (2012).

Chapter 1 of this monograph explored how first Oswin Oswald and then Clara Oswin Oswald sacrificed themselves before Clara came into the Doctor's life on a more permanent basis as the 'impossible girl'. We learn in *The Name of the Doctor* that each of these characters are facets of the same person.

Also explored in the first chapter of this work is the character of Danny Pink, and the unusual nature of his death for **Doctor Who**. We learn that Danny's death is not entirely final. As we see in *Dark Water / Death in Heaven* (2014), he is one of billions on Earth caught in the elaborate trap set by Missy in league with the Cybermen. Part of the plot is to upload the souls of the dead to the Nethersphere. Later, his earthly remains are resurrected as a Cyberman, but he manages to break through the Cyber-conditioning to challenge Clara on who she

---

[175] Tulloch and Alvarado, *The Unfolding Text*, p57.

thinks she is. His ability to break through the Cyber-conditioning echoes Oswin Oswald the Dalek and her ability to break through the Dalek conditioning in *Asylum of the Daleks*. It also prefigures Bill Potts being turned into a Cyberman in Peter Capaldi's last season as the Doctor[176], and Moffat's last story as **Doctor Who** showrunner, *Twice Upon a Time* (2017). That final story revisits the themes of transhumanism and cheating death that feature repeatedly throughout the Moffat years.

Clara's death in *Face the Raven* is, for **Doctor Who**, a straightforward tragedy. She emulates the Doctor's heroism in the mistaken belief that if she fails either he or Ashildr will save her. Her choice is in line with the terrible choices her Doctors made, and forced her to make. Her actions in *Face the Raven* are in line with the lies and subterfuge she has participated in and initiated. One critic, Simon Brew, came to the conclusion that:

> 'A harsh thought, then, and one with ramifications. The Doctor, effectively, killed Clara. The Doctor gave her the belief that she could get out of any corner. That she could take on everything in the world and live. In *Face The Raven*, she did that, and in *Face The Raven*, she lost.'[177]

However, two stories later Clara is resurrected by the Time Lords and at the end of *Hell Bent* she joins Ashildr in a TARDIS in which they embark on their own series of adventures. Once again, this harks back to the very familiar themes of death never being quite final in Moffat's **Doctor Who**, but is also different from the fates of Rory,

---

[176] *World Enough and Time / The Doctor Falls* (2017).
[177] Brew, '*Face the Raven* Review'.

Danny and later Bill. Rory's continuing series of resurrections were unique, too, but Danny's death and resurrection as a Cyberman prefigures that of Bill. They both involved the idea of souls being caught and used by the Cybermen in a plot orchestrated by Missy / the Master. Clara, however, has her extended life taken from the moment that exists between her last heartbeat and her death as caused by the Quantum Shade. So, while she lives at the end of *Hell Bent* (and is seen again, through a separate resurrection, at the end of *Twice Upon a Time*), Clara has still died at the end of *Face the Raven*.

Sarah Dollard describes writing the scene of Clara's death as particularly difficult, and not just because of her affinity for the character. She had to capture all the reactions needed: Clara's fear and regret that she can no longer continue to have fun with the Doctor; Rigsy's survivor's guilt; the Doctor's helplessness – he cannot express his grief and rage right there and then. There is also Ashildr's pain that Clara sacrifices herself uselessly because her plan actually would have meant Rigsy's survival and the Time Lords still receiving her gift of the Doctor[178]. Emily Asher-Perrin's summarised views on the episode capture just how Dollard succeeded in writing the scene:

> 'Perhaps most important of all, she died saving the life of one good friend. Because we're so accustomed to companions doing extraordinary things in the Doctor's name or their own, that we forget how important it is for them to do the subtle, smaller things that good people do. Her farewell is a perfectly constructed scene, allowing the two of them only enough

---

[178] **Writing Who** episode 10, *Face the Raven* DVD.

time to say everything that matters without filters. Every second has to count.'[179]

Face the Raven is the first of three stories that conclude the 2015 season of **Doctor Who**. It sets up the plot and many of the narrative themes covered in the next two stories, *Heaven Sent* and *Hell Bent*, the subject of the next two Black Archives.

---

[179] Asher-Perrin, 'Let Me Be Brave'.

BIBLIOGRAPHY

Books

Aaronovitch, Ben, *Rivers of London*. London, Gollancz, 2011. ISBN 9780575097568.

Aguirre, Manuel, *The Closed Space: Horror Literature and Western Symbolism*. Manchester, Manchester University Press, 1990. ISBN 9780719032073.

Arnold, Jon, *Rose*. **The Black Archive** #1. Edinburgh, Obverse Books, 2016. ISBN 9781909031371.

Bergson, Henri, *Time and Free Will: An Essay on the Immediate Data of Consciousness* (*Essai sur les données immédiates de la conscience*). 1889. FL Pogson, trans, London, Swan Sonnenschein, 1910.

Berston, Paul, and Colin Richardson, eds, *A Queer Romance: Lesbians, Gay Men and Popular Culture*. London and New York, Routledge, 1995. ISBN 139780415096188.

> Isiling Nataf, Z 'Black Lesbian Spectatorship and Pleasure in Popular Cinema'.

Burk, Graeme, and Robert Smith?, eds, *Time Unincorporated: The Doctor Who Fanzine Archives Volume 2: Writings on the Classic Series*. Des Moines, Mad Norwegian Press, 2010. ISBN 9781935234029.

> Anders, Lou. 'The Doctor's Darker Nature'.

> Carroll, David. 'Death.'

> Groenewegen, Sarah, 'Don't Tell the Sisterhood'.

Cooray Smith, James, *The Massacre*. **The Black Archive** #2. Edinburgh, Obverse Books, 2016. ISBN 9781909031288.

Cornell, Paul, *London Falling*. London, Pan Macmillan, 2013. ISBN 9780330528092.

Cornell, Paul, *The Severed Streets*. London, Pan Macmillan, 2015. ISBN 9780330528108.

Coward, Rosalind, *Female Desire: Women's Sexuality Today*. London, Granada Publishing, 1984. ISBN 9780586084472.

Cranny-Francis, Anne, *Feminist Fiction: Feminist Uses of Generic Fiction*. Cambridge, Polity Press, 1990. ISBN 9780745605272.

Deleuze, Gilles, *Bergsonism*. Hugh Tomlinson and Barbara Habberjam, trans, New York, Zone Books, 1988. ISBN 9780942299076.

Doane, Mary Ann, *The Desire to Desire: The Women's Film of the 1940s*. Bloomington, Indiana University Press, 1987. ISBN 9780253204332.

Dobilli, Rolf, *The Art of Thinking Clearly*. Nicky Griffin, trans, London, Hodder and Stoughton, 2013. ISBN 9781444759549.

Fuery, Patrick, *Theories of Desire*. Carlton, Melbourne University Press, 1995. ISBN 9780522846201.

Gaiman, Neil, *Neverwhere*. 1996. London, Review, 2000. ISBN 9780755322800.

Grosz, Elizabeth, *Space, Time and Perversion: Essays on the Politics of Bodies*. St Leonards Sydney, Allen and Unwin, 1995. ISBN 9780415911375.

Grosz, Elizabeth and Elspeth Probyn, eds, *Sexy Bodies: The Strange Carnalities of Feminism*. London, Routledge, 1995. ISBN 9780415098038.

Probyn, Elspeth. 'Queer Belongings: The Politics of Departure'.

Guerrier, Simon, Steve O'Brien and Ben Morris, *Whographica: An Infographic Guide to Space and Time*. London, BBC Books-Penguin Random House UK, 2016. ISBN 9781785940620.

Heidegger, Martin, *History of the Concept of Time: Prolegomena* (*Prolegomena zur Geschichte des Zeitbegriffs*). 1925. Theodore Kisiel, trans, Bloomington, Indiana University Press, 1985. ISBN 9780253207173.

Hourihan, Margery, *Deconstructing the Hero: Literary Theory and Children's Literature*. London and New York, Routledge, 1997. ISBN 9780415141864.

Howe, David J and Stephen James Walker, *Doctor Who: The Television Companion*. London, BBC, 1998. ISBN 9780563405887.

Hutcheon, Linda, *The Politics of Postmodernism*. London and New York, Routledge, 1989. ISBN 9780415280167.

Jerome, Fiona, *Tales from the Tower: Secrets and Stories from a Gory and Glorious Past*. London, Think Books, 2006. ISBN 9781845250263.

Kahneman, Daniel, *Thinking Fast and Slow*. London, Penguin Books, 2011. ISBN 9780141033570.

Kofman, Eleanore, and Elizabeth Lebas, *Henri Lefebvre: Writings on Cities*. London, Blackwell Publishers, 1996. ISBN 9780631191889.

Lefebvre, Henri, *The Production of Space* (*Production de l'Éspace*).

1974. Donald Nicholson-Smith, trans, Oxford, Blackwell, 1995. ISBN 9780631181774.

Lewis, CS, *The Magician's Nephew*. **The Chronicles of Narnia** #1. 1955. London, Fontana Lions, 1980. ISBN 9780006716679.

Miéville, China, *Kraken: An Anatomy*. London, Pan Macmillan, 2010. ISBN 9780330492324.

Monmonier, Mark, *How to Lie with Maps*. Second edition, Chicago, University of Chicago Press, 1996. ISBN 9780226534213.

Pedley, Paul, *Essential Law for Information Professionals*. London, Facet Publishing, 2011. ISBN 9781856044400.

Penley, Constance, Elizabeth Lyon, Lynn Spigel and Janet Bergstrom, eds, *Close Encounters: Film, Feminism and Science Fiction*. Minneapolis, University of Minnesota Press, 1991. ISBN 9780816619122.

> Sobchack, Vivian. 'Child/Alien/Father: Patriarchal Crisis and Generic Exchange'.

Penley, Constance and Andrew Ross, eds. *TechnoCulture*. Minneapolis and Oxford, University of Minnesota Press. 1991. ISBN 9780816619320.

Platt, Marc, *Lungbarrow*. **Doctor Who: The New Adventures**. London, Virgin Publishing Ltd, 1997. ISBN 9780426205029.

Poe, Edgar Allen. *The Portable Edgar Allan Poe*. J Gerald Kennedy, ed, 1945. London, Penguin, 2006. ISBN 9780143039914.

Purser-Hallard, Philip, *Dark Water / Death in Heaven*. **The Black Archive** #4. Edinburgh, Obverse Books, 2016. ISBN 9781909031401.

Russell, Gary, ed, *Repercussions*. **Doctor Who Short Trips**. Maidenhead, Big Finish Productions, 2004. ISBN 9781844350483.

Tasker, Yvonne, *Working Girls: Gender and Sexuality in Popular Cinema*. London and New York, Routledge, 1998. ISBN 9780415140058.

Tulloch, John, and Manuel Alvarado, *Doctor Who: The Unfolding Text*. London and Basingstoke, Macmillan Press, 1983. ISBN 9780333348482.

Warrick, Patricia S, *The Cybernetic Imagination in Science Fiction*. Cambridge MA, MIT Press, 1980. ISBN 9780262730617.

Whatling, Clare, *Screen Dreams: Fantasising Lesbians in Film*. Manchester and New York, Manchester University Press, 1997. ISBN 9780719050671.

Periodicals

Lauzen, Martha M, 'Sisters of the Sitcoms'. *Television Quarterly* vol 28 #4, 1997.

Osborne, Peter, 'The Politics of Time'. *Radical Philosophy* #68, 1994.

Sax, Boria, 'The Tower Ravens: Invented Tradition, Fakelore, or Modern Myth'. *Storytelling, Self, and Society* vol 6 #3, 2010.

Tulloch, John, 'Dr Who: Similarity and Difference'. *The Australian Journal of Screen Theory* #11 & 12, 1982.

Television

Blake's 7. BBC, 1978-81.

Weapon. 1979.

Doctor Who. BBC, 1963-.

    More Than 30 Years in the TARDIS. BBC Video, 1993.

    The Complete Series 9 DVD box set.

        Writing Who episode 10. DVD extra.

        Doctor Who Extra episode 10. DVD extra.

        'Wil Wheaton Interviews Peter Capaldi and Jenna Coleman'. DVD extra.

Game of Thrones. HBO, 2011-.

Map Man. BBC, 2004-05.

    Mrs P's A-Z. 2005.

Film

Allen, Woody, dir, *The Purple Rose of Cairo*. Jack Rollins & Charles H Joffe Productions, Orion Pictures, 1985.

Qu, Vivian, dir, *Trap Street* (*Shuiyin Jie*). 22 Hours Films, 2013.

Web

'Ashildr'. BBC **Doctor Who**.
http://www.bbc.co.uk/programmes/profiles/4JQcjYZB9Nc95cM60Jt L6g3/ashildr. Accessed 22 November 2017.

'Common Raven'. *National Geographic*.
https://www.nationalgeographic.com/animals/birds/c/common-raven/. Accessed 25 November 2017.

'National Statistics: Asylum'. Home Office, 27 August 2015.
https://www.gov.uk/government/publications/immigration-

statistics-april-to-june-2015/asylum. Accessed 23 November 2017.

Asher-Perrin, Emily, 'Let Me Be Brave: **Doctor Who** – *Face the Raven*'. Tor.Com, 23 November 2015. https://www.tor.com/2015/11/23/doctor-who-face-the-raven-review/. Accessed 5 February 2018.

Avia, 'Raven Symbolism and Symbolic Meaning of Ravens.' *What's Your Sign?* http://www.whats-your-sign.com/raven-symbolism.html. Accessed 10 February 2018.

Brew, Simon, '**Doctor Who** Series 9: *Face the Raven* Review'. Den of Geek, 21 November 2015. http://www.denofgeek.com/tv/doctor-who/37920/doctor-who-series-9-face-the-raven-review. Accessed 5 February 2018.

Britt, Hugo Edward, *The Beasts of Battle: Associative Connections of the Wolf, Raven and Eagle in Old English Poetry.* PhD from the School of Culture and Communication Faculty of Arts, The University of Melbourne. June 2014. https://minerva-access.unimelb.edu.au/handle/11343/43159. Accessed 10 February 2018.

Cooper, Jon, '**Doctor Who**: *Face the Raven*, TV Review – Fans Left Reeling by Shock Ending to Gothic Emotional Rollercoaster'. *The Independent*, 21 November 2015 22:00 GMT. http://www.independent.co.uk/arts-entertainment/tv/reviews/doctor-who-face-the-raven-tv-review-fans-left-reeling-by-shock-ending-to-gothic-emotional-a6743601.html. Accessed 5 February 2018.

Dollard, Sarah, '**Doctor Who** Series 9 Episode 10 "Trap Street": Purple Script'. 22 June 2015. BBC Writersroom, November 2015.

http://www.bbc.co.uk/writersroom/scripts/doctor-who-sarah-dollard. Accessed 5 February 2018.

Dollard, Sarah, '"My dream is to be a screenwriter (especially for **Doctor Who**). Do you have any advice?" Yes it turns out I do.' Sarah Dollard's Tumblr; BBC Writersroom 17 November 2015. http://www.bbc.co.uk/blogs/writersroom/entries/af949e90-4979-4525-b3ee-ba48391b738c. Accessed 5 February 2018.

Dollard, Sarah, *Carrion Laughing*. Tumblr. http://carrionlaughing.tumblr.com. Accessed 10 February 2018.

Dollard, Sarah, @snazdoll. Twitter. https://twitter.com/snazdoll. Accessed 12 February 2018.

Gee, Catherine, '**Doctor Who**: *Face the Raven* – Clara Dies, So Will Maisie Williams Be The New Companion?' *The Telegraph*, 23 November 2015. http://www.telegraph.co.uk/culture/tvandradio/doctor-who/12009689/doctor-who-face-the-raven-tv-saturday-clara-what-time.html. Accessed 5 February 2018.

Gibbens, Sarah, 'Ravens Hold Grudges Against Cheaters'. *National Geographic*. Published 6 June 2017. https://news.nationalgeographic.com/2017/06/ravens-memory-unfair-trade/. Accessed 25 November 2017.

Hawkes, Rebecca, 'Why Are There No Female Writers on **Doctor Who**?' *Daily Telegraph*, 9 October 2014. http://www.telegraph.co.uk/culture/tvandradio/doctor-who/11151320/Why-are-there-no-female-writers-on-Doctor-Who.html. Accessed 25 November 2017.

Hines, Ree, '**Doctor Who** Recap Season 9, Episode 10, *Face The*

Raven: Clara Oswald's Finest Hour Is Her Last'. *Forbes*, 21 November 2015. https://www.forbes.com/sites/reehines/2015/11/21/doctor-who-recap-season-9-episode-10-face-the-raven-clara-oswalds-finest-hour-is-her-last. Accessed 5 February 2018.

Holdsworth, Rachel. *Trap Streets Are Real, And Here Are Some of London's*. Last Updated 19 October 2016. **Londonist**. https://londonist.com/2015/11/london-trap-streets. Accessed 23 November 2017.

Jacobs, Frank, 'Help Find London's Missing Map Traps!' Big Think. http://bigthink.com/strange-maps/where-are-londons-missing-map-traps. Accessed 23 November 2017.

Martin, Dan, '**Doctor Who** Series 35, Episode 10: *Face the Raven*'. *The Guardian*. Saturday 21 November 2015. https://www.theguardian.com/tv-and-radio/tvandradioblog/2015/nov/21/doctor-who-series-35-episode-10-face-the-raven. Accessed 5 February 2018.

Matthias, John, and Vladeta Vuckovic, trans, 'The Battle of Kosovo: Serbian Epic Poems'. Kosovo.net. http://www.kosovo.net/history/battle_of_kosovo.html. Accessed 10 February 2018.

Maxwell, Rebecca, 'Map Traps: Intentional Mapping Errors to Combat Plagiarism'. GIS Lounge 7 July 2014. https://www.gislounge.com/map-traps-intentional-mapping-errors-combat-plagiarism/. Accessed 23 April 2018.

Montanari, Shaena, 'We Knew Ravens Are Smart. But Not This Smart.' *National Geographic*. Published 13 July 2017. https://news.nationalgeographic.com/2017/07/ravens-problem-solving-smart-birds/ accessed 25 November 2017.

Mulkern, Patrick, '**Doctor Who**: *Face the Raven* Review – A Pedestrian Dramatic Cul-De-Sac with a Poignant Dead End'. *Radio Times*, 21 November 2015. http://www.radiotimes.com/news/2015-11-21/doctor-who-face-the-raven-review-a-pedestrian-dramatic-cul-de-sac-with-a-poignant-dead-end/. Accessed 5 February 2018.

Ruediger, Ross, '**Doctor Who** Recap: Tattoo You'. *Vulture*, 21 November 2015. http://www.vulture.com/2015/11/doctor-who-recap-season-9-episode-10.html. Accessed 5 February 2018.

Smedley, Rob, '**Doctor Who** Season 9 Episode 10 Review: *Face the Raven*'. Cultbox. 21 November 2015. http://cultbox.co.uk/reviews/episodes/doctor-who-s09e10-review-face-the-raven. Accessed 5 February 2018.

Thomas, Kaitlin, '**Doctor Who** *Face the Raven* Review: Swan Song'. TV.com. 22 November 2015. http://www.tv.com/news/doctor-who-face-the-raven-review-swan-song-144804544376/. Accessed 5 February 2018.

White, Barbara, 'Ferrers, Catherine (1634–1660)'. *Oxford Dictionary of National Biography*, 2004. http://dx.doi.org/10.1093/ref:odnb/73927. Accessed 5 February 2018.

BIOGRAPHY

Sarah Groenewegen BEM has written numerous essays on **Doctor Who**, gaming, and being queer. She obtained her Master of Arts (with Honours) from the University of Western Sydney in 2000 by researching into **Doctor Who** and its fans. Her first novel, *Daughters of Earth*, was published in 2017 in the **Lethbridge-Stewart** range published by Candy Jar. In 2016 she was awarded a British Empire Medal for her services to law enforcement and LGBT+ diversity.

Coming Soon